FIGHTING WOMEN

Interviews by Isabella Lorusso

2020 editing and design
by Rowan Tallis Milligan, Neil Birrell
and Rob Ray

This first edition
printed 2020

ISBN
978-1-904491-35-4

Published by
Freedom Press
84b Whitechapel High
St, London
E1 7QX
freedompress.org.uk

GLOSSARY

BOC (Bloc Obrer i Camperol): Worker-Peasant Bloc. Anti-Stalinist party that merged with communist/Trotskyist dissidents to create POUM.

CNT (Confederacion Nacional de Trabajo): Anarcho-syndicalist trade union and main anarchist faction during the Spanish Civil War. Suppressed by Stalinists in 1937 May Days coup.

ICE (Izquierda Comunista de España): Dissident Trotskyist group led by Andrés Nin Pérez. Dencounced by Trotsky, it merged with BOC to form POUM.

Falange: Political wing of the fascists.

FIJL (Federaction Iberica de Juventudes Libertarias): Libertarian Youth federation. Its Catalan wing was the JJ.LL (Juventud Libertarias).

Mujeres Libres: Anarchist womens' organisation.

PCE (Partido Communista de Espana): Pro-USSR party. Its effective Catalan wing was the PUSC (Partilo Socialista Unificado de Cataluna).

Popular Front: The coalition which formed the 1936 Republican government.

POUM (Partido Obrero de Unificacion Marxista): Anti-Stalinist communist party and fighting force formed in 1935. Suppressed in 1937.

PSOE (Partido Socialista Obrero Espanol): Socialist Party, major faction in the Popular Front. Linked to the UGT trade union. Led by prime ministers Largo Caballero (1936-37) and Nuan Negrin (1937-39).

IR (Republican Left): Social-democratic faction, led by president Manuel Azaña.

UR (Republican Union): Fourth largest party in the Cortes and IR ally.

An editorial note: Nomenclature can be a little confusing when talking about this period. For example, supporters of the Stalinist USSR referred to themselves as communists, as did supporters of the rival dissident Trotskyist organisation POUM. This led to the Stalinists being labelled as Communists (as in Communist Party members), while communists from other factions, and in general, are lower case. Similarly, supporters of Spanish republicanism, often doing so as a broad front effort to fight fascism, were not necessarily the same thing as the Republican government in the Cortes, or members of the Republican Party.

CONTENTS

Glossary		4
Foreword by Beatriz Gimeno		5
Introduction and Prologue		11
Pepita Carpena	Anarchist	15
Manola Rodriguez	Communist	53
Blanca Navarro	Anarchist	61
Suceso Portales	Anarchist	69
Teresa Carbó	POUM	77
Concha Perez	Anarchist	87
Teresa Rebull	POUM	101
Cristina Nin	Catalan feminist	121
Maria Manonelles	POUM	135
María Teresa Carbonell	POUM	153
Pilar Santiago	POUM	159
Conclusions		178
Aknowledgements		180
Afterword by Elisabeth Donatello		181

ABOUT THE PERIOD: 1936-39

In July 1936 a military coup was launched by nationalist military officers aiming to eradicate revolutionary elements in Spain. Led by first Emilio Mola and later by General Francisco Franco, they were opposed by a Popular Front coalition pledged to defend the Spanish Republic.

An armed defence against the coup, made up of a chaotic and often competing mix of anarchists, communists, socialists and democrats, initially held the line but was destroyed through a combination of internal feuding and external interference.

This took two main forms. On the one hand Franco benefited from a massive influx of arms and fighters sent by his fellow fascist dictators — warplanes from Germany, troops from Italy etc. On the other, European States refused to aid the Republic and Russia, under Stalin's control, sold support only on condition of ever-greater influence for PCE and PSUC, his pet organisations.

Internal stresses in the Republic came to a head in 1937, when on May 3rd the Stalinists stormed the Barcelona telephone exchange, then controlled by the anarchists, beginning an internal coup which saw USSR loyalists seize control of the Republic. It was a pyrrhic victory, as neither Europe nor Stalin offered the support required to win against Franco, and the Stalinists were left to flee or die at the hands of the fascists as they rolled to victory in 1939. Franco ruled until his death in 1975.

Two groups of women are focused on here, the anarchists and POUM, a Trotskyist-inspired group which broke with the former Bolshevik leader and was also repressed in 1937. Lorusso's interview series partly came out of her previous work on POUM and its leader Andreu Nin, which leads the questions in some of the latter part of the book.

FOREWORD
by BEATRIZ GIMENO

Beatriz Gimeno is a writer and feminist activist for LGBT rights. She has published several books on feminism, lesbianism and sexuality along with poetry, novels and short stories. As general secretary of the National Federation of Lesbians, Gays, Transsexuals and Bisexuals she was influential in winning the campaign for same sex marriage in Spain. She has been an Assembly Member for left-wing party Podemos in the Spanish Parliament since 2015 and is head of the Women's Institute.

Women of the past ... who speak to the present.

Isabella Lorusso presented us, a little while ago, with her book *Voces del POUM*, in which she recorded the memories of men and women who were militants in the Spanish Marxist Party (POUM) founded in 1935, which most people haven't heard of, but played a key role in both the so-called Spanish Revolution and the Civil War. The militants, both men and women, of the POUM paid dearly for not giving in to Stalinism and for denouncing, along with the anarcho-syndicalists, Stalin's crimes and doing so, moreover, at a time when Russia seemed to be the only power capable of defeating fascism.

Today, Isabella is capturing other voices and other memories but this time, those of women. The Spanish women who were militants both in the POUM and in the anarchist movement of the 1930s have a lot to tell us. If anyone was to break down those barriers which seemed to be made of cast iron, if anyone in those heady days promoted revolution and also an inner revolution, it was to be these women. They were activists in a revolution which went far deeper than the one which their male working class comrades were involved in. These women were also workers but they were fated to be girlfriends, wives and mothers who had to submit to the church, to look after their homes and their families. And yet they rebelled in a radical manner. They deconstructed themselves and then engaged in a process of rebuilding themselves in a form capable of not only confronting the boss and the church as their fellow comrades were doing but also — and always with pain — their own families. They had to carry out two revolutions ... at least.

For us to have an idea of just how important these women's organisations of the years of the Popular Front[1] came to be it will suffice to point out that the anarchist organisation Mujeres Libres[2] had a membership of nearly 29,000 at a time when the Communist Party membership stood at 25,000. These activists, anarchists, and communists, first had to change themselves, free themselves from the family yoke, the yoke of a Catholic education which was particularly repressive toward women and also the yoke of a traditional culture and they did so by teaching themselves to read, taking advantage of any free moment in the day to learn, by going to classes after a day's grind in the factory, by taking part in political discussions in which they had to unlearn all the disempowering baggage they had accumulated as women — they were hungry to learn. They trained themselves and then they organised themselves politically; then they went to the front, found themselves in Franco's prisons and French concentration camps, were exiled to Mexico. They lived extraordinary lives for women of their age, so very different in every way from the lives of the Spanish women who stayed here where everything was covered in the drab greyness of the Franco years. People often talk of the suppression of political rights under Francisco Franco, they talk less of the suppression of women converted by the regime into mere shadows of those who seized back their own lives.

The republican women fought for their own lives and in the end they lost. But before the defeat they lived a bright and privileged moment. A moment that one of them explains in these words, "It's like when spring arrives and the trees are waiting to explode, you know? And when the leaves unfurl and say hey! Here I am! Well, that's the image I had when I saw those women realise they were wearing a corset that was holding them in and when they threw it off, well, can you imagine the demands they made. The men were dumbfounded. Their journey started with startling their male comrades". These women questioned everything and their voices still surprise us and play on our emotions.

The story of the revolutionary militants of the early 1930s in Spain shows us how hope became a beacon for the oppressed and all that was put into play to gain a dignified life which up till then had always been denied them. They fought in their country and then spread their fight across all of Europe in the fight against fascism. But that story has already been told.

---

1. The banner under which left and pro-Republic groups formed the Republican government of 1936.
2. Female organisation created during the Spanish Civil War. It was founded by anarchist women some months before the beginning of the Civil War and involved republican women in the anti-fascist struggle together with the promotion of women's self-emancipation.

What has not been told is the story of these female fighters, and that is why when we read or hear their stories we cannot but feel how contemporary their voices still are. The words of these ageing women — more than 80 years old — surprise and move us because their dreams are so like ours, the younger ones let's say. And they confirm as well that there are questions where women still seem to be waiting to make progress.

They, like us, had two battles to fight. The one in their own homes. Suceso Portales tells us something that those of us women who are involved in parties, unions, and social movements today know very well:

"It may sound strange, but many comrades, including the anarchists, not only didn't support us, but even hindered our political activity. They couldn't understand why we organised meetings for women only. They believed that we were going to split up the anarchist movement, that we didn't know who our "real" enemy was; they tried to teach us how to be involved in politics at a given moment in time but we were interested in building the future".

They all make reference to the need to fight on these two fronts to make two revolutions: the one public and the other private. In this way the words of Manola Rodriguez, a woman born in 1917, also seem up-to-date: "It was strange to see how our male comrades, who wanted to change the world, when push came to shove they weren't interested, even for one moment, to question their private lives". And Eva reaffirms: "They always fall into this trap! They can say what they like about the capitalist system: that it is unjust, cruel, mean ... but the patriarchal systems brings a glint to their eyes because it puts them in a privileged position which, obviously, they don't want to give up". Manola allows herself, and with good reason, to let today's women know that "they must fight for their rights, which are many, because it is not true that we no longer live in a male dominated, patriarchal society as they would have us believe.

In every corner of the world, in every home, it is the man who is king and he is king even though outside the home he is exploited and oppressed. With respect to 'his' wife, or women in general, he always enjoys a relationship based on power. What we women need to understand is that we need to organise ourselves in a feminist struggle to claim our rights; men will never concede anything that we cannot win but through struggle. As women and as revolutionaries we must engage in two fights. On the streets we may have them at our sides but in the home we might fight them". And that was said by a woman born in 1917! These words can be painful for any of us.

It is also surprising how far they have come in some areas. Educated in a much more repressive and unequal private and public morality, these women were able to reach almost to the point that we have arrived at today. They would seem to have gone through walls of reinforced concrete, breaking it into pieces.

They discussed everything: sexuality, prostitution. They defended a joyful sexuality for women, free love, abortion, contraception. The words which we hear here, in the mouths of women over the age of 90, remind us where we have come from and where we are now. We cannot be surprised that we are facing the same struggles that we are facing the same resistance. With regard to abortion Blanca Navarro says, for example, that "women never needed a law to abort. Obviously, a law which granted the right to abortion was a great achievement for the women's movement, a great recognition of our social and political role. Women weren't just baby factories, but were also militants, soldiers, rebels, fighters". Today when this basic right is being called into question around the world we need do no more than listen to these words.

Because it was these women who made the most radical of revolutions consisting in a need to change oneself first, then one's comrades, and by means of this personal transformation extend it to everything. They gambled on an extreme compromise between their own lives and the streets, between the factories and the schools, wherever there was an anarchist or a POUM militant it was their own lives that were being questioned. They would accept no compromise with the system. They fought each and every one to make of their lives a personal and political compromise,

"For them the revolution began at home, in the factory and in the town. They didn't baptise their children and they didn't impose any ideology on them. These things may seem trivial to you but they are not. How many people are really ready to organise their lives and those of their children in order to perpetuate their faith and ideals in which they believe? In contrast with the collective silence and general conformity they stood out because they questioned their private lives and their day to day existence".

The women whose voices come out of this book were not only involved in a revolution to change themselves and their male comrades they were also involved in the revolution which aimed to change the balance of power in the Spain of the 1930s. And the story they tell must serve us today when we find ourselves at a time when a vicious neo-liberalism is condemning millions of people to poverty and throwing millions of lives on the rubbish heap.

These militants were persecuted, imprisoned, murdered in many cases by those who pretended to be their comrades in arms. As one POUM militant says, "It was a terrible time because everyone was against us: the government, the socialist party, the Communist Party, everyone ..."

And when war came they wanted to send women home to look after the kids, but they had had a taste of freedom and wanted none of it, "They didn't realise that it was such an important thing and they put it to one side. They thought: the war is here and there are more important problems than the question of women. They didn't understand it was all part of the same picture". But the women had figured it out and they fought for their freedom until the end.

I wish to end with an anecdote which one of the anarchist women, Pepita Carpena, tells and which for me sums up perfectly the spirit not only of this book but, above all, the spirit that enthused these women, "against everything," a spirit which transcends and which is made from a thirst for justice and against conformity but which is also forged from the desire to never give up ones own thinking nor one's own humanity to never let it fall into another's hands:

"When I was a girl I had a childhood friend who was in the youth group where we met up. Then when I went to live in Hostafranc I lost sight of him and I met up with him again, during the revolution, on the Plaza Caluya when I was coming out of work and we hugged each other. 'How are you? What are you up to?' I asked. 'Nothing much, I'm in the Communist Party,' he said.

"And that gave me a nasty feeling which I could see bothered him and he said: 'If the Communist Party ordered me to kill you, you who are my friend, I'd do it.' I was surprised because he really meant it. I said to him: 'If the CNT told me to kill you I wouldn't do it. Firstly, because I can't see why the CNT could want me to kill you and secondly because I have enough of a mind of my own to judge things for myself. Are you not ashamed?'

"This is a true story. It happened to me personally".

The work being done by Isabella Lorousso to bring us the voices of these women and men so that they should not be lost is priceless, because today we need to listen to these voices more than ever.

~ Beatriz Gimeno

INTRODUCTION & PROLOGUE
by ISABELLA LORUSSO

Those who deal with oral history must always go on tiptoe into other people's lives. It is easy to hurt the people interviewed, even involuntarily, with useless or impertinent questions.

When two people meet it is always an act of love. Empathy is needed to choose, at the end of the interview, what to transcribe and what should be left on the tape. Discretion is crucial, because in an informal environment, you may talk about some sensitive issues from the past and things may be said that should not be written.

However, despite wanting to do so, it is impossible to report everything on paper. In fact, anything can make a difference: the location, the situation, the sympathy of the listener, the insight of the interviewer, the colour of the walls or the ring of a telephone.

When you get in touch with people who have gone through extraordinary events such as war, hunger, repression, exile, you feel unworthy, because it is impossible to compare our daily miseries with the pain of those who really wanted to change the world.

This collection of interviews talks about emotions enriched with historical memory. There is a transversal and direct gendered vision, together with the urgency to know and understand and the desire to communicate.

Just like any book of oral history it has its faults, but its strength is the enthusiastic research by means of the stories, words, looks, emotions and empathy, intended as the ability and the desire to "put oneself in the others' shoes," being aware of the fact that it is impossible to actually be in someone else's shoes, as we are not and will never be in another person's skin.

***

It is impossible to separate the history of the female members of the POUM from that of the men who were members of that party. Although historians tend to analyse the women's struggle and isolate it from its historical context, this approach is particularly difficult when it comes to the POUM and the women who were part of it.

The female section of the POUM was established during the civil war and dealt with literacy courses, fought against prostitution, provided nursery schools and soup kitchens.

These tasks were not easy, especially during the struggle against hunger, war, fascism, but also against fathers, husbands, brothers, and comrades.

Many women put their life at risk for the revolution, such as Mika Etchebéhère, a young captain of Russian origin who, after the war, moved to Paris; the Austrian Katia Landau, who started a hunger strike in prison; Pilar Santiago, who devoted herself to painting in Mexico; Teresa Rebull who became a world famous popular singer; Teresa Carbó, who at the age of 102 still used to say, "The Stalinists tortured me because I had seen Nin[1]. But I don't regret what I did. Why should I regret it?"

Then there were also the anarchist women who joined Mujeres Libres: 20,000 women who came from every corner of the country to fight against any kind of abuse or gender, race or class discrimination. In order to interview them, I had been travelling for many years and in many ways to Catalonia, France, and Italy. I was welcomed into their homes and I shared with them endless struggle.

Lucía Sánchez Sarornil, Mercedes Comaposada, and Amparo Poch y Gascón were the three founders of this extraordinary feminist group.

The Irish historian Mary Nash said of them in the introduction to her book *Mujeres Libres*: "The Mujeres Libres members were anarchists and did not limit themselves to claim their rights as women, but also fought for their emancipation as well as for the social revolution, namely for freedom, equality and mutual support through the autonomy of all the human beings".

Many of them left for the front, while others kept working in the factories or dedicated themselves to political propaganda in the cities. After the defeat and the ensuing exile most of the historical memory has been lost, but some of it has fortunately been recovered over the years.

I had the chance to meet Suceso Portales and Pepita Carpena, the anarchist female founders of Mujeres Libres and women who chose to shoulder a rifle and fight on the battlefield, like Manola Rodriguez who belonged to the maquis, the guerrilla groups who fought during the 40 terrible years of the Francoist dictatorship.

In the Pyrenees I met Cristina Simó, granddaughter of POUM leader Andreu Nin, which completes the collection.

---

1. Andreu Nin Pérez, a POUM politician who was arrested by the Stalinists during the 1937 May Days Stalinist coup on charges of collaborating with Franco and then tortured to death.

There is so much left to be said and let's hope that history will still talk about us. After 17 years, I decided to put an end to my collection of interviews with the belief that this end may be a new beginning and that the beginning will never end.

~ Isabella Lorusso
Lisbon, January 5th 2013

PEPITA CARPENA
(1919-2005)
ANARCHIST | Interviewed March 1997, Marseilles

From Bezier, my friend Marta Vergonyós and I made our way to Marseilles to interview Pepita, who issued propaganda for the Mujeres Libres feminist group. We were so amazed at what we learnt at that meeting that we continued to talk about it for many years. Then I returned to Italy and Marta to Catalonia, where we kept Pepita's wonderful dream of love and freedom alive.

ISABELLA: Hi Pepita. I would like to ask you some questions.

PEPITA: OK, let's start.

ISABELLA: When did you start getting involved in politics?

PEPITA: I don't remember the precise date because I was very young. I used to spend a lot of time with my grandmother who supported the Republic. She was a revolutionary although in other ways she was very traditional. She was a woman of her time and there were many sides to her.

ISABELLA: You say she was a revolutionary, but she wasn't very active politically was she?

PEPITA: She was always ready to intervene whenever there was an injustice. When I was a child I was a rebel. As soon as I began to go to mass I realised that there were injustices there as well. The Spanish church was very fanatical. Spain was the country where the highest number of churches were burnt down by people because when people revolt the first thing they attack is that which has done them the most damage. I wasn't ready for all that praying stuff. I attended a school run by nuns. It was called El Surtidor, in Calle de Blasco de Ramay which is still there today. We were forced to recite the rosary and Hail Mary most pure every day. I learnt many things, but, based on my experience, I don't like Catholic schools. Then I went to another school but we were made to go to church on Sundays there as well. To check they would ask us what colour the priest had been wearing. It could have been one of several colours. So we took it in turns to go and we would tell the others the colour so we didn't all have to attend.

MARTA: When were you born?

PEPITA: I was born in 1919, and I started working at a very early age when I was just 10-12 years old. There were lots of strikes. My father was a bricklayer and my mother had to work to make ends meet. One day, I went to a factory called "la tigre" on Plaza del Doctor Letamendi which produced raincoats and was looking for workers. I was not even 14 and child labour was forbidden, but I applied anyway without telling my parents. I started working as an apprentice. I learned how to sew. At school nobody checked for absences. At the end of the week I took the money to my mum and said, "Take it". My mother was so surprised. "Where did you get the money?" "Don't be surprised — I have found some work". "How come?" "I have left school and started work because I can't bear the way things are at home".

Very emotional, she began to cry and made a gesture I will never forget. She said, "If you really want to work, and I am not forcing you to, I want you to learn a profession".

She knew that I liked tailoring — as a child, I used to make clothes for my dolls — so I began to work as an apprentice. I was 12 years old, maybe even younger because, in April 1931, when the Republic was formed I was already working in Calle de la Cucuruya with the Fonbernats — a brother and sister.

They had a brother, Joseph, was a deputy and also first violinist at the high school, a truly Catalan and progressive family. I liked working with them.

ISABELLA: Did you leave school?

PEPITA: Yes. I just knew how to read and write and I wasn't good at maths. I've always liked writing.

ISABELLA: How long did you stay with the nuns?

PEPITA: I only stayed there for a short while, because the school was increasingly expensive. I was the oldest, then my brother had to study as well and there was not enough money. From Calle Blai, where I was born, we moved to Pueblo Seco.

ISABELLA: Do you remember anything about your relationship with the Church?

PEPITA: I remember an episode about the priest who celebrated the marriage ceremony of my mother. The priest was self-righteous and questioned the virginity of my mother, but my grandmother answered harshly, "The Pharisees would have sent you away from the temple with a rifle!" And this is precisely how that poor sod died! During the war he was shooting from the bell tower and the republicans killed him. It may sound cruel but, at that time, many priests took the side of the coup organisers.

I witnessed the greatest injustices at the workplace. At that time, apprentices did everything and I also worked as a maid. They treated me well but paid me half rate. The male CNT members used to carry out propaganda activities and I took an interest in them. My father was a staunch supporter of theirs. He said they did everything they did for the good of the people and who faced up to everything at risk of going to prison in spite of their precarious family condition. Later, I realised that militants shouldn't really have a family. You can't allow your children to have to face the consequences of your activities. Am I not right?

At that time, the only leisure activity for the youth was dance and I used to go to the ballroom with my aunt. The girls who danced sat in the front row and those who accompanied them in the second or third one. I didn't like this as I realised that the girls had to wait for the boys to choose the one they fancied the most. As soon as I joined the feminist movement I understood what this was all about. I realised that women were just like slaves waiting for someone to come along and choose them.

MARTA: As if you were in a shop window.

PEPITA: Yes, yes — like a shop window. It was almost a form of prostitution. You just stood there waiting for someone to come and pick you with a macho attitude: I like her, I don't like her. I have always been self-confident and a good dancer, and when you are a good dancer, your physical appearance and your partner don't matter at all. You simply have to know how to dance.

Once I went dancing with my aunt's sister-in-law, "Pepita, please, take her with you otherwise she won't be allowed to go out". I started dancing when I was 12 years old and, on a Saturday night, I went dancing to the Parallelo near the port. This place had a bad reputation. There was a certain promiscuity. But on Saturday nights it was attended by respectable people. When the music suddenly stopped your partner had to give you a gift. So I received a lot of cups, spoons, porcelain items and so on. It was called the "baile del ramo".

Then there was a kind of lottery, the "tolla", and the boy who won offered the prize to his girl. This was the most emotional part of the dance. I hope that these words will help you understand the situation of women in that period. It was 1933, I was just 14 years old and the CNT men came to the ballroom to talk politics to us.

They asked us, "Do you know that there is a trade union that defends your rights?" So I went to the trade union and asked what it was all about. "We are concerned with social issues," they answered. "Well, I'm interested in social issues," and so I stayed with them.

ISABELLA: Did this happen during the dance?

PEPITA: Yes, during breaks. These CNT members went to the places attended by the youth to get their attention. They went to the ballrooms, libraries, beaches, everywhere ... They did a great job.

Girls never paid for the dances, and this was good, because we had no money. The working lads paid for both of us. Then I thought, "If we are having fun together, why should it only be the men who pay?" They regarded women as mere ... objects to be displayed. The more attractive the girls were the more successful the dance would be.

Beautiful girls attracted boys who paid for the dances. This was a tradition of the 1930s. One day, I applied to the trade unionists and said, "I want to learn". And they answered, "On that day, in that place, there will be an assembly at that time. If you are interested come along". So I did. I didn't know then that a trade union could have different sections, which is rather logical and natural today, but how could I figure out then that this was so important?

ISABELLA: Was your father an anarchist, too?

PEPITA: No, he liked the CNT men, like other people in the village. They were very appreciated because they represented a good example. In 1936, during the first days of the revolution, there was nothing but the CNT.

MARTA: In your family, who was your political influence? Maybe your grandfather?

PEPITA: No, I had no political influence at all.

MARTA: And what about your grandmother?

PEPITA: She wasn't a political influence. She was a rebel. She was left a widow when she was very young and had to face life all alone. However, she was a conservative, traditionalist woman, just like my mother. For example, one day I gave up going to mass, because the priest asked me morbid questions, he wanted to know what I did with boys. I was shocked because I hadn't even thought of such things. I told him I didn't do anything like that with the boys. So I told my mother I wouldn't be going to church any more.

ISABELLA: Did you have any brothers or sisters?

PEPITA: I was the oldest, then there was Pasqual, who was two years younger than me, and Anita, who was named after my mother and died of meningitis. The workers' children died of illnesses that were not treated. Then I had another brother, who was ten years younger than me but by that time we had moved to another district.

I liked the meetings because nobody had ever talked to me about things that were important to me personally. That is to say social issues. I didn't know that they existed! It was 1934, I was 14 years old, and I enrolled in the trade union there and then. I went there and said whatever came to my mind without knowing that there were rules to be followed. One day, a comrade said: "Pequeña, ("Little," that was my nickname), I really like the things that you say, but there are some rules, there is an agenda, there are some topics to be discussed," and then I understood how it worked.

Thanks to that dance, I got in touch with the trade union and soon understood that injustices were everywhere. I learnt a lot of things with the trade union. I attended the meetings of the trade union but I had no important tasks. However, I liked it so much that I used to spend a lot of time with them after work. I worked in Calle de Porta Ferrada, I would cross Las Ramblas and went to Santa Monica, where the trade union office was. One day, a comrade approached me and asked me what I was doing there. I could see he was intrigued that a young girl was there as there were not many women involved, especially in the metalworkers' union. Perhaps he thought that I was the daughter or sister of a member of the trade union.

MARTA: As always happened.

PEPITA: Yes — exactly. And he asked, "Girl, do you have work?"
I replied, "If I'm here, it means that I'm working?"

"OK, what's your job then?"

"I'm a tailor".

"A tailor? What are you doing here in the metalworkers' union?"

"I'm here because I'm interested in the CNT, the social struggle".

And he said, "You should go to your trade union where they will surely need your help, it is in 30 Calle del Carmen".

So I eventually found the right place, where there was much work to be done. There were the great struggles of the textile industry. At that time, women were exploited in a terrible way, there were many meetings.

There I became a militant. My comrades accepted me happily despite my young age. It wasn't like now with the reformist trade unions which have corporate committees that negotiate with the company owners who generally call the shots. The owners are the ones in charge. The current trade unions have sold their souls: a trade union with corporate committees is no longer a trade union. In the past, trade unions went to the company owners and said, "We've come here on behalf of the workers to negotiate these issues: salaries are inadequate, working conditions are unfair and these things must change". I accompanied them and learned a lot of things as I focused on their approach to the company owners. They were incredibly hard and focused.

The trade unionists used to say, "We are talking in a civil and polite tone but if the problems are not solved we'll take tough actions". And if the owner kept on exploiting the workers we blew up an area of the factory and, the following day, the owner was ready to meet our requirements. We were not violent by nature, we were forced to be violent. When you learn about an abuse, then what do you do? No one defended us! I have experienced the struggle first-hand. Now I'm not working, I cannot argue about it, if I were unemployed, maybe I would make concessions. I don't know, maybe, but it is not in my character. So, in 1934-36 I began to be a militant, then 1936 arrived. At that time, I used to go out with a boy who had been my boyfriend for many years ... he also became an active member of the CNT.

ISABELLA: What was his name?

PEPITA: Pedro Pérez Mir. He was a mechanic and belonged to the metalworkers' union. He was on the strike committee and all sorts. He was active in his section and I in mine.

MARTA: What was your task in the textile trade union?

PEPITA: Initially, I dealt with registrations, then I took care of other things that have to be done in a union as well. I didn't have any great responsibility because I was very young. I did attend committee meetings.

ISABELLA: Did you talk about the repression of the Asturian miners in 1934?

PEPITA: Actually, I was very young. So I found out about a lot of things some time later. I knew that most of my comrades had been imprisoned and negotiations were conducted to set them free.

ISABELLA: This happened in 1931, during the First Republic.

PEPITA: Yes. The trade unionists said, "We should not isolate ourselves, we must involve young people so we can strengthen the union". One day, a comrade said, "Oh Pepita, can you imagine our joy when we got out of prison, went to the trade union office and saw so many young people?" It was amazing: we thought that our struggle had not been useless.

ISABELLA: Were there also members of the Communist Party?

PEPITA: Well, I didn't know them. I met them during the war. But before then I didn't even know that there was a Communist Party. I kept on attending the textile trade union but I still loved the metal industry one, which my partner had joined, so I joined the Libertarian Youth of the metal industry, with all the consequences which militancy entailed in 1934-1936. The union knew that the right wing was laying the foundations for a coup, while the government was not aware of it, since Azaña[1] provided no weapons and did nothing, but why? Because they were corrupt! They were helping Franco, and if people had not protested, we would have been repressed by fascism. The comrades used to say that there would be a coup. In 1936, before July 19th, the trade unions were joined by many young people, because they knew that something was going to happen. I used to sleep at the headquarters of the metalworkers' union and thought, "If something happens, I must be ready to get involved and do whatever needs doing". Helping the injured, cooking and attending meetings. The metalworkers' union was based in Rambla Santa Monica, in front of the military barracks.

---

1. Manuel Azaña (1936-40) was prime minister of the Second Spanish Republic and a leading organiser of the Popular Front.

When the coup took place, the comrades immediately gathered in the streets. Most of the soldiers were doing military service and didn't want to hurt us. Conversely, the professional soldiers used to wildly shoot at us, while others said, "How can I kill my brother?" This happened on July 19th-22nd. The putsch in Catalonia was put down and then we found out who was willing to jump on the bandwagon, such as the socialists and the same Catalanists. They were more moderate at that time and asked for more independence while remaining within the Spanish union. This was 1936, I was about 16, since my birthday was in December. That was the story of my militancy until the death of Ascaso which was very painful for me because I knew him personally as was also the case with Durruti[1].

At that time, you could be imprisoned simply because you were a member of the CNT. They met in Calle San Pablo, near the Parallelo, where there was a café called "Pai-pai". Upstairs there was a ballroom. The CNT members of the metalworkers' union used to meet there. One day they were all arrested. My partner was in prison for nine months simply because he had a CNT document. This is how we used to live.

Then there were the elections. The CNT generally suggested abstaining from the vote but that time didn't give any indication, because it hoped that the left wing would set our imprisoned comrades free. And this eventually happened, even if it didn't last. During the "two black years" there was a cruel repression and the "escape" principle was applied: they used to say, "You are free, you can go". And when they did, they were shot in the back for attempted escape. It was horrible! They have made films about all that stuff.

I'd like to tell what I experienced first-hand during the revolution, and I'm talking about a revolution, not a war, because the revolution in Spain was a clear fact. In 1936, there was a congress in Zaragoza which established the rules to be followed in case of a revolution, which meant that we were ready to fight. As soon as I joined the trade union, I realised that education was really necessary. In addition to social struggles, the CNT men were interested in culture. There were debates among the members of the Libertarian Youth, the most educated ones taught things to the others. What I enjoyed the most were the discussions. During a meeting, someone would say, "Read such and such a book", and at the following meeting the participants talked about that book. At that time the most popular authors were the French ones: Rousseau, Zola, Balzac. Those of you who have attended school lessons cannot imagine what this meant

---

1. Francisco Ascaso and Bueneventura Durruti were perhaps the most famous anarchists involved in the initial defence of Barcelona. Ascaso died on July 20th 1936, Durruti on November 20th while defending Madrid.

for us. We were mostly illiterate or semi-illiterate because reading and writing are not enough. We gradually acquired a social culture within the trade union, together with general notions based on the books of famous writers, which turned out to be important in our life.

So, despite the criticisms made of the CNT men in relation to women's liberation this movement has actually urged many people to study and this is important. There is a girl in the video (*De toda la vida*), have you seen her? She is Ortensia Torres and says that at school they were forced to lie to pupils although they didn't want to.

In 1936, we witnessed an important event that was very painful for us — the Communist counter-revolution of May 3rd 1937. The anarchists were part of the government, although we mostly opposed it; however, this happened under some specific circumstances: we had no choice, what else could we do? I don't know if we were right, I still don't know. But if we had given up, what would have happened? Maybe a dictatorship. And anarchists don't want any dictatorship. This is the reason why there are Stalinists, isn't it? And today people may say of us, "You were as Stalinist as them," and this isn't good.

ISABELLA: But being a member of the government and being Stalinist are not the same thing.

PEPITA: I know it's different.

ISABELLA: The contradiction was that the Catalan government was made up of four anarchists. Federica Montseni, minister for health; García Oliver ... How could an anarchist become minister for justice?

PEPITA: And García Oliver made big mistakes. He died in America after having written a book which I criticised in an article that I wrote!

ISABELLA: Why did you criticise him?

PEPITA: Because he is selfish and if you read his book you are left with the impression that he made the revolution all by himself. And he also criticised his friends, like Durruti, and I don't like this. However, I am going off at a tangent.

ISABELLA: Oh no, not at all. What does the revolution mean for you? I'm asking because you said you have to live a revolution.

PEPITA: I supported the Spanish Revolution because those who dealt with organisation, those who gathered in Zaragoza, put into practice what they had promised. During the revolution, the economic trend was positive. In Spain, qualified workers were as skilful as the engineers, and this happened even in my profession. During the revolution, thanks to the workers, communities did very well. And how could governments accept such great results? Simply they couldn't. But we were so enthusiastic, to the extent that we believed that this situation would last forever. I am talking about us younger ones.

ISABELLA: Were the factories self-managed as well?

PEPITA: Yes. Even the wood and textile manufacturers. They were collectivised and socialised. Even hairdressers were collectivised. Many were surprised by the fact that the people could manage the economic life of the country and this frightened them. Later there were excesses when churches were burned to the ground — this happened because the people were sick to the back teeth with the Church. I think that we must respect others' views within a democratic system but we have our limits. We have an example at the moment about a film which is out which deals with the life of Christ and there are those who want it banned because it is offensive to the image of the Church. I ask you!

MARTA: During the civil war, did you stay in Barcelona?

PEPITA: Yes. I stayed with the trade union. Then I went to a factory because it was looking for workers. It produced grenades and other war equipment. I started to work there with a comrade of mine.

MARTA: Did you manufacture grenades?

PEPITA: Yes, grenades and other things. I left my job as a tailor because my boss escaped to Venezuela and it was hard to find employment. There were job advertisements in the newspapers, but there were many applicants. However, I also worked elsewhere as a tailor. I was hired immediately, because I was skilful.

ISABELLA: When did this happen?

PEPITA: It was in 1936. I used to work hard. I was always busy, attended meetings and still led my usual life. That was when we learned about the first communist and socialist women: they were good at political strategies. They suddenly sprang up like mushrooms, while the Mujeres Libres group already existed in 1936. They had emerged three months before the beginning of the revolution, but they had a long history going back. They had even conducted a survey and knew that their movement would get the support of society in general at that time. Spanish women were sick of being treated like slaves. Successo Portales, Lucía Sánchez Saornil and Amparo Poch met in Madrid and the Mujeres Libres group was founded by them. In Catalonia, the group was established by Soledad Estorach and Concha Liaño, and I joined them at a later time. Mujeres Libres is worth being considered separately.

I have already told you that I started working at a factory and it was there that I met the women of Mujeres Libres who were looking for new militants. I believed that men and women should fight together. I wasn't interested in a female movement. This is how it should be from a logical point of view. As it happens, within the anarchist movement, there is no distinction based on gender, social class, race or whatever. But theory and practice are not the same thing and human beings are not infallible. I'm especially referring to men — whether they are anarchists or not, they are all the same. At that time, I had not yet joined Mujeres Libres. My partner was at the front and sometimes returned to Barcelona and worked as a mechanic in a workshop called "Garage Durruti". I became a member of Mujeres Libres when the Libertarian Youth appointed me as its representative at the local federation. I worked at Paseo de Gracia no. 20, which, during the revolution, was the headquarters of the SIA national committee. And there I met Lucia Sánchez Saornil and a secretary called Mary who used to work hard. They were arranging for a regional meeting which should decide upon the establishment of a female secretariat. I didn't like this idea because I believed that men and women should join forces without any separation.

ISABELLA: There was a lot of machismo in that period, wasn't there?

PEPITA: Yes, undoubtedly. At that time, during the revolution, many women wanted sexual liberation as well. I think that there should be no differences between men and women also from a sexual point of view. One day, a guy who belonged to the Libertarian Youth told me, "You act like a libertarian, but if I ask you to have sex with me, you won't go with it". Luckily, I was quick on the draw and replied, "I have sex only with the men that I like and I wouldn't kiss your mouth for all the money in the world!" I was so upset that I eventually left and added, "from now on,

I will work only with women". I left the Libertarian Youth and joined the women. There I met Mercedes Comaposada, who was a true inspiration for me, I esteemed and loved her so much. She was a skilful pedagogue; do you know this? She died in Paris some years later, I always remember her.

We immediately dealt with prostitution, we looked for jobs for those women who wanted to give up this "profession". When I joined the group, they were already well organised, so I became a member of the central propaganda committee which operated in the region. I worked with Agueda Abatio and this experience really opened my mind. Considering the mindset in Spain at that time, after eight centuries of Arabian domination, the strong machismo, the fact that men wanted to rule over women, who — in their opinion — could just have children and take care of their family, the creation of a female group during the social revolution was amazing! So I gave up the libertarian movement and devoted myself to women's issues, because everyone had innovative ideas, but at home they behaved even worse than the others. Too much lip service had been paid to these issues but the facts were staring us in the face. When I was a member of the metalworkers' union, there were lots of meetings but there were almost no women, so I asked my comrades, "Have you got a partner?" And they answered, "Yes, of course!" And I asked, "Why isn't she here with us?" And they explained, "Because she is at home with our children". And I said, "Oh that's not a problem. Next time, you can stay at home and she can attend the meeting". So they would say, "Ah, you are ahead of your time!"

So I joined Mujeres libres to issue propaganda. We went to underdeveloped villages and met many women.

MARTA: In the provinces?

PEPITA: Yes, in the provinces. We started in San Vincente and then moved across Catalonia.

MARTA: And how were you welcomed by the local women?

PEPITA: We already let things be known before our arrival. We said that we were going to organise a meeting with Mujeres Libres and invited all the women. They had so many brilliant ideas that it gave me goosebumps. It's like the onset of spring, when the trees are full of blossom. This is what they looked like: it seemed as if their emotions had been locked inside a corset and then they suddenly started to flow outside. This happened during the war. Now I don't want to go on about this question, because a tragedy happened in May. I don't want to talk about the fight between the militants, because it was horrible, everyone was against us: the government, the Socialist Party, the Communist Party, and so on. They joined forces against us because of what happened at the telephone exchange.

ISABELLA: What was it like to live in that period?

PEPITA: Communists wouldn't let the anarchists manage the communication lines for the whole of Catalonia. They started to protest and that is when it all began. Someone blamed the CNT members but actually the Stalinists attacked the exchange. Tension grew and we began to build barricades. I stood behind a barricade in Calle San Paolo, in the Rambla. They shot from Plaza del Pino, from the Iglesia del Pino. It was the Communists who were shooting, there were many dead and hundreds of wounded. Such a counter-revolution during the revolution was shameful.

ISABELLA: There were more than 500 dead.

PEPITA: Many, too many dead. And even Berneri[1] was killed. He heard a noise but couldn't escape; they took him and killed him. There was also a friend of his whose name I don't remember. They killed a lot of people.

ISABELLA: In your opinion, why did the Stalinists do this?

PEPITA: Because they blindly obeyed orders from Moscow! They took gold from Spain to Russia and promised that they would give us weapons in return. But those weapons were ... I can't describe them. My partner knew them very well, because he was fighting on the front. Those weapons were useless and had been sabotaged so that they couldn't be used. They said the anarchists were no good at fighting but rather it was because they had no weapons. The weapons were all assigned to the communists. The communists used to hide their weapons and sabotaged those destined for the others. Therefore, the factories controlled by the CNT started to manufacture their own weapons and equipment. But it was too late. Stalin sent a terrible Russian consul: he tried to repress anarchy by any means,

---

1. Camillo Berneri was an extremely influential theorist and writer who was expelled from Italy by Mussolini and fought on the Aragon front. He was assassinated by the Communists on May 5th 1937.

but failed, because we were many. Thus, the communists, the socialists, the Stalinists joined forces: they wanted a dictatorship of the proletariat, but we didn't agree, do you understand this?

ISABELLA: Even Largo de Caballero recalled from office Oleg Orlov, the Russian consul of Barcelona, after the events of May.

PEPITA: And then he was sent away and was replaced by Negrín. Theirs was a political campaign. Our approach was different and when they ordered us to lay down our arms we did it with the utmost pain. But if we had already known about those who were killed we wouldn't have given up the struggle and there would have been a bloodbath. Many people were arrested, including a friend of mine from the metalworkers' union who disappeared.

My comrades called me and said, "Pepita, the Communists have taken him, we have to check and find out if he is in one of the establishments under their control". So I went to all the places controlled by the Communists and said: "What a beautiful place!" A Stalinist replied, "I'll show you around". They took the Pedrera, occupied the best premises in Barcelona. We had beautiful places as well, but we avoided the eye-catching ones, after all we didn't care about luxury and marble. Eventually, after having visited some offices, I saw a storage closet with bars and some prisoners inside it. I recognised my friend but acted as if nothing had happened. I warned my comrades and they immediately went there looking for him.

ISABELLA: In your opinion, why was the repression of the Stalinists mainly directed at the POUM militants instead of the anarchists?

PEPITA: The repression was maainly directed at the POUM, because they (the Stalinists) didn't agree with Trotsky[1] and then the POUM members joined us. The POUM actually already criticised Trotskyism, since they realised that this was not what they were looking for and the Stalinists did what they used to do in Russia: attacking the anarchists and the Trotskyists. This was how Stalin operated!

ISABELLA: They killed Andres Nin as well.

---

1. Lev Davidovic Trotsky was a senior Bolshevik during the Russian Revolution. Leader of the Red Army from 1918-25, during which time he oversaw the repression of Krondstadt, he fell foul of Stalin in the late 1920s and was forced into exile. He remained influential theorist and was killed on Stalin's orders in 1940.

PEPITA: Yes, Andres Nin was a member of the POUM.

ISABELLA: Federica Montseny and Garcia Oliver[1] played an important role in bringing an end to the events of May 1937.

PEPITA: Yes, they tried to bring peace. If the Communists had continued their struggle, there would have been a massacre, and if we had caught the Communists, we would have killed them. I'll tell you an anecdote.
 One day, I met a friend of mine on Plaça de Catalunya, of whom I had lost sight, and he told me that he had joined the Communist Party. I shuddered and replied, "I'm an anarchist!" "An anarchist? Well, if the Party orders me to kill you, I will do it". He had become a fanatic, so I answered, "If the CNT orders me to kill you, I won't do it ... shame on you!" I didn't see him again, but I've told you this anecdote to help you understand how the Communists took so many young people and turned them into murderers. He was an old friend; his name was José. These things helped my personal growth. As soon as I joined the Mujeres Libres group, I became a militant feminist. With them I completely devoted myself to the women's struggle and politics, I used to go from one village to another to issue propaganda. Sometimes we drove with our CNT comrades, one acted on behalf of the FAI, another one on behalf of the Libertarian Youth and I on behalf of Mujeres Libres. So they helped us, we joined forces. We travelled throughout Catalonia; I didn't know it so well at that time. It is hard to explain all the work that we did. There were some hardships, but Mercedes Camposada[2] trained us to fight.

ISABELLA: What do you mean?

PEPITA: Before issuing propaganda, we attended some courses. We discussed some topics, for example: women as women, mothers and workers, we had a good understanding of feminism. We didn't accept that men considered themselves superior to us. Sometimes there was a sort of competition among us: "I want to be an engineer because women are just as capable of being engineers". NO! I want to be an engineer simply because that is what I want to do. "I like being a woman. I like it when the men look at me. I don't want to be a scarecrow!" I'll try to make myself clear: emancipation must be achieved gradually; you mustn't allow anyone to stop you. With Mujeres libres, I visited the militia.

1. Montseny was an anarchist who became minister of health in 1936. Olivier was minister of justice.
2. Camposada, also known as Mercedes Guillén, was an anarchist theorist, fighter, author who co-founded Mujeres Libres. She survived the war and outlived the regime, dying in Paris in 1994.

ISABELLA: On the front of Aragon?

PEPITA: Yes. My boyfriend was at the front, his name was Pepe. One day, I visited him and he said, "Pepita, stay here for some days, will you?" I hesitated, but then I thought, "If they want to put me on trial, I won't run away!" There the battle of the Segre and then the battle of the Ebro broke out, and Pepe was killed. I knew nothing more about him, I don't even know where he was buried. They sent me his documents when I was in exile, but I lost them on the road. I only know that he was buried in a village called Moncayo, but I don't even know if it really exists. Initially, they told me that he had been wounded in his stomach by the enemies' machine guns, so I looked for him in all the hospitals. My comrades accompanied me and then one of them told me, "Let's go to Manresa, there is a list of the dead there". He went there and found his name in the register. It was horrible for me, because I had known Pepe since I was a little girl. We even got married because Pepe loved my parents! I initially said no, because I was a rebel and kept saying, "No, I don't want to marry you". And he replied, "Your father will be happy, what does it matter if you have a civil registration?"

So some comrades of the 121st division obtained a licence and we celebrated together. They loved us. Pepe and I had a party at Juan's house, a friend of ours who lived on the Rambla. That house still exists you know. It is on Rambla de Santa Mònica, near the port. They arranged for a party for me but I said, "We have got married, but nothing else has changed for me".

ISABELLA: Did you get married in 1937?

PEPITA: No, in 1936. Before leaving for the front. He said, "We must get married, I don't want to leave you like that". No, ... it was not in 1936. It was at the beginning of 1937. And he died in 1938. We stayed together for such a short period! It was a tragedy.

ISABELLA: Were there also women at the front?

PEPITA: Not many. At the front, women had ordinary tasks: we talked to the militants, brought them soap, cards, something to eat, we spent some time together and encouraged them.

MARTA: Did you meet any woman who was on the front as a militant?

PEPITA: The only militant that I met was Concha Pérez [Interview: page 87]. I might have left for the front, but I didn't like weapons. When I went to the front to visit my partner, Durruti used to ask me, "Pequeña, what are you doing here on the front? Don't bother us, eh?" Then, with Mujeres Libres, we organised some soup kitchens for the militants. I did so many things that I cannot even remember.

ISABELLA: What do you think about the fact that Durruti didn't want women on the front?

PEPITA: Durruti was a great man.

ISABELLA: Was he from Barcelona?

PEPITA: He was born in León but joined the Barcelona metalworkers' union. I met him when I was 14. He was in prison with my partner. When I thought about the possibility of fighting, I used to ask myself, "What am I going to do behind the barricades?" I'm afraid of bullets, but I'm not a coward. Simply I cannot stand the idea that a bullet may kill a person, even if it is inevitable sometimes.

ISABELLA: But many women wanted to leave for the front and Durruti hindered them.

PEPITA: This is not true. Actually, many prostitutes went to the front.

MARTA: And Durruti said that women had to leave the front because they had venereal diseases and were infecting the militants.

PEPITA: Yes: not all the women were prostitutes, but he gave this order to preserve the militants who were not infected. It's like when you go to the surgeon: sometimes, to remove a sick limb, you must give up a healthy one as well. It was not fair, but his purpose was to avoid the spread of the infection.

MARTA: Blanca Navarro told us that men were often ill and infected women.

PEPITA: Yes, this might be true. But I don't know much about this, because I didn't experience it first-hand. For example, the film on Mujeres Libres or "Land and Freedom" shows how women fought at the front. If I had been at the front, I would have done what I had to do. I would have fulfilled my duties. And nobody could have said that I was a prostitute, however I don't think that I would have been able to kill someone, even at war.

MARTA: And what do you think about the fact that Durruti prevented women from fighting?

PEPITA: I didn't agree because it was a sort of segregation against women. Moreover, many women left the brothels and didn't know where to go. Maybe some of them left for the front. There were some peaceful moments there, when nobody shot, and we just relaxed and did nothing. But men must learn to control themselves. Perhaps some of them were irresponsible. I don't know. I cannot judge, because I wasn't there. If Durruti had sent them away, evidently he despised them, didn't he? I knew Durruti, and I don't think that it was a matter of contempt — it was a considered decision.

We must take into account the context of that time to be able to judge. I heard of women who had joined the female secretariat with me and then were ashamed of having become members of women's groups, such as Encarna Jiménez, the secretary of the organisation. Now she says that she doesn't remember anything about that. It's crazy!

ISABELLA: Have you watched the film *Land and Freedom*?

PEPITA: Yes, and I liked it very much, although it doesn't deal with anarchists. Loach was a POUM supporter and a sincere man. When the film was released, I went to the debate and said that the scene when the militant killed the militia woman was exactly what the Stalinists did in Spain. I was really moved by the film. I cried from start to finish.

ISABELLA: And what did Loach tell you?

PEPITA: He said, "I don't deserve Pepita's compliments. I congratulate her and all those who defended the Spanish Republic. I have just told true stories in a film". This was Loach's reply.

ISABELLA: We would like to ask you something about Mujeres Libres.

MARTA: When you joined the group, had the prostitution project already started?

PEPITA: Yes, it had already started.

ISABELLA: Do you remember any particular anecdote of the time when you were a member of the group?

PEPITA: There were some training schools which taught some professions. Prostitutes attended nursing classes, while others went to school for the first time. I met a woman who gave up prostitution, had a love affair with a militant and became an excellent comrade; I saw what happened to her first-hand.

MARTA: The results were positive.

PEPITA: Yes, of course. It's worth stressing that the Mujeres Libres group was established in Madrid before the war by Conchita Liaño and Soledad Estorach[1]. They were few but their numbers increased. We even organised a national meeting. In 1936, during the revolution, we had a great organisation.

ISABELLA: Was the meeting held in Valencia?

PEPITA: Yes, it was in Valencia. Many branches of Mujeres Libres arose in Catalonia and all over the country.

ISABELLA: Why was this group established?

PEPITA: These women fought on behalf of all the others. This was amazing and we didn't understand why the CNT initially didn't support us. And it was the first women's group. It was established to provide training courses to uneducated women. Everyone could join the group. There was Amparo Poch y Gascón who was a doctor and a paediatrician and almost all the group organisers were intellectuals.

The Catalonian ones were trained but had no special qualifications, they were neither journalists nor intellectuals. The group had an incredible impact on society. I know this for sure because I dealt with propaganda.

---

1. Liaño joined the Libertarian Youth aged 15 and was a founder of Mujeres Libres, editing its newspaper. She was the inspiration for protagonist Concha Liaño in the film *Libertarias*, though was critical of its portrayal. Soledad Estorach Esterri was a key early organiser who helped found Grup Cultural Femení, a precursor to the Mujeres Llbres. She worked on construction teams, as a care and canteen organiser, and as a representative of FIJL. She collaborated on the production process of *Land and Freedom*.

We talked to women in a clear and direct way and suggested discussion topics. They were fed up with being subjected to men's power.

MARTA: Do you think this can be regarded as working-class feminism?

PEPITA: Yes, and it was different from the English "suffragettes". They were "high-class", rich women. There were many feminist groups, but this was the only one led by female workers.

MARTA: Based on interviews with other women, we have realised that they considered themselves female and not feminist.

PEPITA: Yes, that's true. Feminists had an extremist attitude, because they wanted to be separated from men; "female" means women who struggle for their emancipation without this leading to any separate group. As for feminists ... there were also cases of abuse.

ISABELLA: Yes but there are many types of feminism.

PEPITA: I know. Here, in France, we took part in a meeting and there we noticed the difference between the female and feminist movement. There were women from Italy, France, Spain and other countries. The meeting was called "Anarchy and Feminism". I don't remember the year but it was in Lyon. We had the chance to analyse the difference between these groups and ours.

ISABELLA: There are different ideas about feminism. Marta and I witnessed the movement of the 1970s and regarded ourselves as feminists.

PEPITA: One day, a friend of mine called me and said, "There is a meeting of a group of women. Please, come, but do not bring Moreno, because men are not allowed to participate". "Then don't count on me," I replied. "If Moreno cannot come, I won't come!"

MARTA: But this separation was present also in the Mujeres Libres group. Your activity was carried out exclusively by women.

PEPITA: We also accepted men but actually nobody came.

ISABELLA: Did men write articles for your newspapers too?

PEPITA: Yes, of course. They could feely express their thoughts and we were glad to see that they supported us.

MARTA: And what were men's reaction to Mujeres Libres? Women joined forces and became aware of their situation; but what did men do?

PEPITA: I think that they were scared.

MARTA: Do you remember any anecdotes?

PEPITA: I believe that they didn't understand us and made fun of us. Sometimes, they called us Mujeres Liebres, "hares" as a sign of their contempt.

ISABELLA: What do you mean?

PEPITA: What do hares do? They run. The wanted to say that Free Women were libertine, like prostitutes. It was a distorted view of the reality. This movement was established before the revolution, that is the reason why we were trained and ready to fight. Our movement was innovative. Most of our partners were at the front to fight against the supporters of the Falange[1] and didn't understand that our movement was important too. "There's a war on and there are problems which are more important than the women's question," they used to say. They didn't realise that it was all interconnected.

MARTA: Yes, also because Mujeres Libres made arrangements for nurseries and canteens.

PEPITA: Yes, and women drove cars and trucks, they did everything. They organised so many things and faced so many challenges. Then other women wanted to jump on the bandwagon just to catch the others' attention by raising their fists and waving flags. But we did the most important things for women in Spain. Thanks to this movement, I realised the importance of the women who founded it.

---

1. Falange primarily refers to Falange Española, a Spanish political party which merged with the Juntas de Ofensiva Nacional-Sindicalista. A socially conservative nationalist movement with fascist leanings, Falangism under its founder Primo de Rivera advocated a "national syndicalist" economy which rejected both capitalism and communism. When Franco took control the Falange became Spain's sole political party and abandoned its anti-capitalist tendencies, becoming a tool of the Caudillo's own conservatism.

ISABELLA: In your opinion, men and women should fight together, so why did they establish a movement only for women?

PEPITA: Because in Spain the condition of women was very tragic. Women were totally subjected to men. At home, for example, the macho had all the rights, and the woman took care of everything. Men did nothing. Now boys and girls help each other with the housework. Women were despised, they were useful only in bed. And if you are just a sexual object then you don't deserve anything.

MARTA: And what differences were there between Mujeres Libres and the other groups of women, like the women's secretariat?

PEPITA: The difference lies in the fact that when you join the Libertarian Youth, there are men and women who share the same idea of the world, and this is specified in the statute. However, many women decided to create a specific movement because women didn't express their thought at meetings if men were present. It was not a matter of separation; they just wanted every woman to feel free to express herself.

MARTA: We call this feminism. Women should be free to talk and exchange ideas.

PEPITA: Yes, because some women could not talk if there was a macho. And when Emma Goldman[1] came to Barcelona she was surprised by the macho attitude of many CNT male members towards women and said, "I cannot believe that the CNT men have this outdated view of libertarian women".

ISABELLA: Why did she say so?

PEPITA: She realised that they were backward-looking. She came to see what the revolution had achieved and she realised that the comrades feigned ignorance on serious problems.

MARTA: But you said that both the Youth and the CNT did not recognise the activity carried out by the Mujeres Libres group.

---

1. Goldman was one of the most influential anarchist figures of the 19th and early 20th centuries. A prolific writer and orator in her native US, she was a tireless campaigner for the republicans during the war.

PEPITA: Actually, they recognised it, there was a sort of siblinghood, however, it was just an informal recognition, not a political one. We often prepared flyers together but the writing on the posters was CNT-FAI and never Mujeres Libres. We have never been able to reach this goal. They did not regard us as a brother-group.

ISABELLA: Yet your movement was strong, membership was more than 20,000.

PEPITA: Yes, and our statute stated that when Mujeres Libres disappeared all our goods would be entrusted to the CNT. It was clear that we were with them but evidently it was not enough.

MARTA: Besides the flyers, when activities were organised or support was needed, how did you notice the absence of such recognition?

PEPITA: They supported us, but it looked like a favour, we wanted a real recognition. It was not a matter of rejection: they gave us cars, and everything we asked for. But we wanted to be considered an autonomous political entity, a group of adult women who knew what they wanted. And since our spokeswoman was Federica, we fell out of the frying pan and into the fire! Do you understand what I mean?

ISABELLA: No, are you talking about Montseny?

PEPITA: She underestimated us. She pretended to support us but did nothing for the women's movement. And I thought: a woman like her, an avant-garde feminist, wrote books where she expressed her ideas, however, she also said things that didn't mean much to me.

ISABELLA: Can you give an example?

PEPITA: She said that childless women were like trees without fruit. Well, nobody should say that especially a woman like her! And she said this only because she had three children. And what does this mean? I'm fed up with discussions about children.
   Some comrades of mine used to say, "Anarchist blood flows in my veins". This is very stupid! Anarchy is not hereditary! Anarchy derives from a revolutionary attitude, from the willingness to fight against injustices; you are an anarchist if you choose to be such, right? You cannot be an anarchist

just because your father was one, do you understand? Obviously, the son of an anarchist is more likely to become an anarchist as well, but there are also opposing influences, like, for example, anarchist parents with fascist sons. These topics are poorly debated: the effect of a libertarian education on children and why in our society women are unfairly segregated.

ISABELLA: This happens all over the world.

PEPITA: Yes, of course. Once I attended a meeting on anarchy in Venice and a Swedish girl told me that she was surprised by the fact that I had radical ideas about feminism because of my age, and I replied, "I am not the only one, because my "ancestors" started the liberation of women. Women like Flora Tristán, Clara Zetkin, la Kollontai[1], who were forward-looking with reference to both syndicalism and socialism". And this gave rise to an amazing debate. It took place in the square and was more useful than the discussions held at the meeting place.

ISABELLA: More interesting and more informal.

PEPITA: Yes, more informal and more intimate. She hugged me and said, "Pepita, in spite of your age, the way in which you face issues related to women really inspires me". I couldn't believe it! I thought that in Sweden the condition of women was better.

ISABELLA: Yesterday you said that you met Federica Montseny during a conference.

PEPITA: Yes, it was a conference on issues relating to women. Some of them opposed mixed organisations and Federica said that she didn't want any separation. This is what she used to say. She said that we had to fight together and there was no reason for separation. And how can you fight if you have so many prejudices? Her idea was to defend first ourselves, and then the others, and this is what I told her, "Your words sound good because you come from a family that taught you how to become a leader. The comrades respect you and recognise your skills, but when you talk about the condition of women, you're wrong. Because there's a big gap between theory and practice".

---

1. Tristán (1803-1844) was a French-Peruvian socialist, Zetkin (1857-1933) a German Maxist and Alexandra Kollontai (1872-1952) was a Russian revolutionary who became the most prominent female member of the Bolshevik government before her internal criticisms led to the party sidelining her.

When Federica was speaking, no one dared interrupt her, but this did not happen with the other women. Thus, the Mujeres Libres group was created, precisely because this problem was not solved.

ISABELLA: I guess she wasn't happy hearing your comments.

MARTA: Yes, but the strangest thing is that she, as an anarchist, had become the minister for health; at that time, a decree on abortion was approved, wasn't it?

PEPITA: Yes, it happened at that time, but she did nothing. Mujeres Libres forced her to draw up that decree. It was not her achievement, it was an initiative of Mujeres Libres. And so abortion became free in Catalonia.

ISABELLA: This happened in 1936, is that right?

PEPITA: Yes, in 1936.

MARTA: Can you tell us the story of some comrades of yours who benefited from this decree to abort freely?

PEPITA: Well, the girl who came to France with me had just aborted. She got pregnant and aborted at the hospital during the war. In 1936 there were many abortions.

ISABELLA: And where did women abort before then?

PEPITA: Before then, abortion was illegal but if you were rich, nothing would happen to you, like now. We are looking at the past instead of moving ahead. Now I'll show you an article that I wrote in 1977 after Franco's death. It says that parliament was preparing a new law on freedom of expression, freedom to divorce, freedom for political parties, but did nothing against the law on adultery. "We hope that freedom will prevail in this reactionary state," this is what I wrote. Then I also wrote the following about a factory.

Forty women were fired, and, at the urgent request of the trade unions, they were reinstated. To punish them, the owner of the factor forced them to face a wall for a fortnight and they, in turn, told their story to Radio Barcelona. We still had a lot work to do with regard to women's rights in Spain after the dictatorship. Under the democratic regime, after Franco's death in 1977, there was still a dictatorship from many points of view. Now I'll read an article published in a newspaper, "The militant Pepita Carpena, in exile for 40 years, has never given up the fight that she began with Mujeres Libres. Things have just slightly changed in the last 40 years, including the relationship between men and women and between fathers and children. The following text is the unpublished story of the struggle of a free woman". Here is what it said:

"The need for a specific female movement was very strong in 1936, thanks to the feverish political and social activity during the civil war. However, many women had already become aware of their condition of slavery, both as workers and as women, and started to join the CNT movement, which represented the most appealing ideology. This is the reason for their name, Mujeres Libres, which means women without prejudice. Our trade union struggle continued with the FIL[1], where we discussed all the problems concerning the status of women, including sexual and social issues. Culture covered most of our activities, because at that time only a few women were able to study, while most of us could just read and write. Almost all the women from the age of 12 had to work. The conditions of the workers were so miserable that we managed on our own to learn the basic ideas that we were unaware of. Most of us joined Mujeres Libres and believed that men and women should fight together.

"The most urgent struggle concerned the workers, and we had to fight in our own area of competence, at home, in our daily environment. We had to eradicate the prejudices resulting from so many years of Christian education. We joined the trade unions as militants, however, the total emancipation of the individual was an entirely different story.

"Unfortunately, our comrades, who were good militants, put the issues of women aside, stating that women weren't able to understand problems. Their attitude was condescending. They behaved as if they were doing us a favour. During our discussions, we clearly realised the separation between men and women was due to prejudices which were difficult to be eradicated.

"This criticism also applied to our youngest libertarian comrades. There are so many stories about this that I could tell you and so many misunderstandings about our discussions of free love. Young women, fed up with all the chains that oppressed them, were amazed

---

1. Federacion Iberica Libertaria — Iberian Libertarian Federation

at the power of liberation. Many people gathered in the universities and on trade union premises. We had a lot of work to do during our revolution. In 1937, during a FIL congress, it was decided to establish a women's group despite many of us opposing the move, because there was already a movement of women called Mujeres Libres, founded by Lucia Sánchez Saornil and Mercedes Camaposada.

"Many women still feared to express themselves because of the 'male superiority' of their comrades, something of which the latter were not even aware in some cases. Many militants like me joined Mujeres Libres. Initially, I didn't believe that it was necessary to create a movement of women only, because it looked like a backward move, but later I understood the great importance of this movement.

"In the group we discovered what didn't work and learnt that we were responsible for our own liberation. A period of discussion was followed by significant progress; what women asked for and obtained in 1937 was what we had already predicted in 1936.

"It should be remembered that the government of the Republic granted women the right to free abortion, while in France this happened only in 1976. The struggles of these extraordinary women who gave everything to support the movement have not been given the attention they deserve, because the CNT comrades have always tolerated but never fully appreciated us.

"At the time of the war, with all the political struggle that was going on, what was regarded as secondary was put aside. However, it is impossible to deny the important role of women in their families, both as a partner and as an individual.

"But our strength has raised the women's awareness in our group, and many of them understood that emancipation depended on them. Thanks to our struggle we had already made great advances, which had allowed our young comrades to be more integrated and understood. The new generation involved both men and women in the struggle: what yesterday seemed impossible and inconsistent today seems normal, and it's almost normal to talk about the prejudices which we had met during our journey. Therefore, many women became militants".

Then the article refers to a meeting held on June 2nd in Barcelona, which was attended also by Federica Montseny and another member of Mujeres Libres, or rather a comrade. During the meeting many women took the floor, and I was proud and glad to see the results of our efforts.

"However, many of our comrades could not overcome their long-standing superiority complex. These four lines will clearly explain our struggle to let the work carried out with perseverance and strength by our comrades be positively received in order for the condition of women to increasingly improve over time.

Our comrades have neglected this issue, but I'm sure that things will change. Political parties have understood this and have put the issues relating to women at the centre of their focus, using women for their political interests. Maybe they are actually interested, but surely exploit women. We must be consistent with our libertarian ideas but, actually, these things shouldn't even need to be discussed. The simple fact that we talk about them means that something still doesn't work as it should; if we raise the questions honestly and draw the proper conclusions, we'll make a step forward towards revolution".

ISABELLA: Your words have inspired new questions. For example, when you joined the Mujeres Libres group, did you stop attending mixed groups?

PEPITA: I was involved in loads of things, but when I started to devote myself to the women's struggles, then I had no more time to spend on other things up to my retreat.

ISABELLA: Was your retreat due to lack of time or to other reasons?

PEPITA: Only to lack of time. However, the women's struggle excited me and I was surprised by women who knew things beyond my imagination, and I threw my lot in with them. However, as I had attended mixed groups as a young girl, I couldn't give up the struggle involving my comrades — our friendship continued.

Just like Federica Montseny, in 1936-37, my comrades have always respected me, and I personally had no problem with them. However, there were many male trade unionists, but anarchy was different; it was not easy to support an anarchist struggle.

ISABELLA: Were there any non-anarchist women in Mujeres Libres?

PEPITA: I think almost all of us came from the CNT. Probably there were those who were just interested in Mujeres Libres, I didn't know everyone involved — there were 20,000 of us. But we had so much enthusiasm; there was something new about us, our work was far reaching.

I gave everything, but I was just one of many, an anonymous girl who had joined Mujeres Libres.

ISABELLA: Yesterday you said that the women who had joined the Mujeres Libres group embraced anarchism and gave up communism.

PEPITA: Yes, clearly. It was a natural consequence of the founders' aim to join the social struggle of the CNT.

ISABELLA: But there were also other anti-fascist women's movements.

PEPITA: Yes, but they had nothing to do with us. Our group was created before the war with a clear standpoint on anarchism. And those women took advantage of the situation in Spain during the revolution. But they didn't really care about women's liberation, it was all put on.

MARTA: There were a couple of lesbian women in Mujeres Libres. Did you openly talk about this issue?

PEPITA: No, we never talked about that.

MARTA: But we knew this, didn't you?

PEPITA: Yes, of course! I knew it and I naively talk about this topic in a video.

ISABELLA: Yes, we saw that video.

PEPITA: And I said to Lisa and Carol, the producers of the video, "I wasn't expecting that issue to come up and now I have made a mess of the matter. Not because I said that there were lesbians in the group, but because I said that Lucia Sánchez Saornil was lesbian". And it was true. I was young and it made an impression on me since she was open about it. In the video, I was talking about lesbians, but then I also added that I had never seen Lucia Sánchez Saornil argue the case for lesbianism. She was just open about it.

ISABELLA: But was it obvious? Did you know about it?

PEPITA: Yes, of course! I saw something different and I didn't realise what it was! I was young and noticed that she was open about it.

And I appreciated her even more, because she was so strong to assert it in spite of everything and everyone. There were prejudices at that time in Spain. She asserted it and was ready to fight.

ISABELLA: Did Lucia want men to join Mujeres Libres?

PEPITA: Yes, she thought that we should fight together. Then we lost the war and retreated; perhaps if this freedom had lasted a little longer, we could have achieved even more.

ISABELLA: In your opinion, if Lucia Sánchez Saornil had publicly declared that she was a lesbian, would she have run any risk?

PEPITA: No, I don't think so. There was much tolerance especially among women, who were more forward-looking with respect to these issues.

ISABELLA: Then why didn't she declare it publicly?

PEPITA: Maybe because it was her private life, although she was open about it. But she never said publicly, "I am lesbian". Because this is a sexual matter and everyone lives their sexuality in their preferred way. This is what I said during a conference on sexuality in Bilbao to an Englishman who asked me, "What do you think about homosexuality?"
He was trying to embarrass me but I replied, "I have my own personal sexuality and I don't think that a trade union is the forum to discuss such issues. This is a place for social struggle. Sexuality is a private matter. If someone is discriminated against because of his or her homosexuality I think that we should give them our support. But we don't need to claim homosexuality.

"I don't discriminate against anyone because they are homosexual, but I am opposed to legal recognition of their relationship".

ISABELLA: But without legal recognition there would be emotional, employment, and social discrimination.

PEPITA: This is what happens with open relationships, there are no rights. For example, I had a problem with my youngest daughter. I didn't get married and I couldn't recognise her until the law changed. I didn't care about laws, she was my daughter in every sense. Sometimes a psychologist came to me and nit-picked. But I sent her away.

ISABELLA: Sara Berenguer said that, during the civil war, people used to get married in an informal way and then there were some problems when they needed official documentation. Would you mind translating the other part of your article from French?

PEPITA: The other article that I wrote dealt with the status of women in 1936-39 in Spain as well as with certain events in the libertarian movement: CNT-FAI-FIL and Mujeres Libres.

"Forty years later, this urges me to consider the current status of women. Everyone knows the terrible repression to which the Spanish people were subjected during Franco's dictatorship, when human beings were worthless. It was impossible to speak or protest. How did women react to this injustice when ancestral laws regarded them as inferior to men? The improvements that we had obtained in 1936 with our struggle had been completely swept away. I'm talking about the law regarding abortion, divorce, and the women's independence. Today, in 1977, I am ashamed of this, but women still depend on the laws enacted by Franco's regime. In Spain, there is a strong machismo, which can be also described as "phallocentrism". Adulterous women may still be imprisoned if they are denounced by their husbands. The opposite situation is not even considered. So men can be unfaithful, but women cannot. In other words, men can fornicate with any woman, while women cannot. Nowadays, in 1977, this law sounds ridiculous in spite of the death of Franco and the support given by democratic parties who protested in the streets. But these laws have not been abolished yet.

"Today women are not considered individuals yet; this regime is a fake, because everything has remained the same. All the establishment institutions reinforced by Francoism hinder anything that may lead to a revolutionary change. The strongest of these is the Church, which exerts a great influence over family life, relationships and moral behaviour. You cannot have a civil marriage, you must opt for the religious ceremony. This was still the case in 1977. Now you can celebrate civil marriage, but it was forbidden in the past. Among the various political groups, I would like to mention Mujeres Libres, which I had joined. Women will play a role in the future of Spain, and today nothing can be done without them. In 1977, many women didn't work, they depended on the salary of their husbands. Women were regarded as servants, sometimes they were loved, but they still remained servants. I don't want to talk about women and work only, because we should consider also the choice of having children, among other things. The free decision of women is the most important thing; life is theirs and they must be allowed to decide to work outside the family and get in touch with other people. Women are not slaves and don't belong to any master. During my travels to Barcelona, I noticed a strong awakening among women; these women still had to face the same taboos, the same prejudices, the same male opposition of 40 years ago.

"I had the chance to talk to many young women full of enthusiasm and new ideas who, perceiving themselves as adult, don't want to be subjected to any paternalism. They need examples, not advice. They suffer from the lack of an intermediate generation, then one which was forced to leave the country and travelled worldwide. After a long exile and 40 years of silence and repression, many women are now going back home, but this return has always been unpopular, I cannot understand why. Our enemies are waiting for the once subdued people to rise and unveil all their lies. The efforts of the Church to silence everything have been useless, since rebellion flows out of every pore, together with the desire to break all our chains. These women must fight against everything and everyone, against these terrible prejudices that regard them as slaves. The radio was just talking about a law on freedom of confession, divorce, and the free establishment of political movements that is going to enter into force. Nothing has been said on adultery yet. Let's hope that freedom will gradually replace repression".

MARTA: This article written in French should be translated and published.

PEPITA: Yes, because it explains the whole history of the movement. My French comrades said, "You know the situation in Spain very well, why don't you write an article that may inspire the new generations?" This is important, because I speak of my experience in the 1930s and compare it with the situation in the '70s, when women in Spain are still subjected to patriarchal power.

MARTA: After the war and exile, were there other groups of Mujeres Libres? In 1961 the newspaper was published again in London.

PEPITA: Sara Berenguer is more informed on this issue, because I had joined the CNT here in Marseille at that time and I was no longer in contact with the other militants. My new comrades were not very motivated, and when I talked to them about Mujeres Libres, I realised that they weren't interested. At that time we were very busy: we organised theatre exhibitions and debates, and were involved in militancy, amongst other things.

MARTA: Did you participate in any publication?

PEPITA: No, never after the war.

MARTA: And now are you still in touch with Sara and the other women?

PEPITA: Yes, with the women in Madrid, like Concha Serrano. We attended a debate in Barcelona in 1993, which is reported on in a book. And in this book there is a chapter entitled "Feminism and post-feminism" on which I collaborated. Take a look at it, it talks about me:

"The experience of Pepita Carpena in the workers' movement as well as in Mujeres Libres during the Spanish war seems forward-looking. The way in which they faced problems needed an independent female organisation while keeping in touch with the political parties and mixed organisations, and this is precisely the difference between the Italian and the French feminists. Their feminist approach questions the family, the ideas of the left wing, men's supremacy in the political and scientific sphere, the attitude of women from the allegedly developed countries. The family still acts as a shelter against the destructive effects of industrial society. The working class is poorly organised and is often exploited by political parties. And, in this context, the women's wish for change is a strong political force that fights against a conservative society".

MARTA: I'm glad to hear that you regard yourself as a feminist, because this word is often intended in a negative way, as evidenced by numerous interviews with the members of Mujeres Libres. They seemed to be afraid to use this word, and replaced it with "female".

PEPITA: It doesn't matter to me, because I clearly know what it means, so I don't need to change it.

MARTA: Feminists are generally regarded as women who reject men, but this is not true.

ISABELLA: Feminism is a huge movement.

PEPITA: Yes! There are so many differences within the movement. Since you have interviewed the other women of Mujeres Libres, what is your opinion?

MARTA: Sara Berenguer said that initially it was hard to be a member of Mujeres Libres because some male comrade of hers laughed at the meetings that she attended. She was fed up with this attitude and decided to join a group of women.

PEPITA: Sara says: "Why aren't woman free to have their own ideas?" Men know that they are free to express their opinions, but they don't want women to step forward and this is unfair. They thought that our movement was illegitimate so they missed an opportunity to focus on themselves.

ISABELLA: We have interviewed a dozen women, but you are definitely the most radical one, the only one who has questioned her private life and political struggle; it is clear that you have revolutionised your life from a theoretical and practical point of view. As a self-taught person, you have taken control your life.

PEPITA: In my life I have always put my ideas into practice.

ISABELLA: Women are often afraid to express their ideas so as not to offend men or maybe to win over them.

PEPITA: Oh, no! I have always been frank with my partner and I've always told him, "This is me, I'm not you. You must accept me for what I am. I cannot change myself to please you". And if I have to fight against him even for some small aspect of everyday life, then I'll do it. I'd rather do this than hide things. It's not a matter of domination.

MARTA: You are translating your thoughts into your daily life and this is amazing.

PEPITA: This is the result of a daily struggle, it's what makes us who we are.

MARTA: You don't look for the approval of others and don't allow anyone to speak on your behalf. It can't have been easy to say those words to Federica at that time, but you did it. Do you remember any other woman, a militant or a founder of Mujeres Libres, who shares your principles and values?

PEPITA: Well, for example Jacinta Escudero, the secretary of the local federation of Mujeres Libres, an upright woman; I lost touch with her. Then there was another comrade of mine who issued propaganda with me. She left Spain, because she was tired of so much pain.

MARTA: And what about the founders, like Mercedes Comaposada?

PEPITA: Our age difference was great. I considered her a pedagogue, a teacher. But I didn't know her well enough to establish a direct relationship with her. Sara was in contact with her because they edited the magazine in London. I thought that she was strong, but then I realised that it was not so, because as soon as she found out that I had said what I did about homosexuality in the video, I had to face a lot of problems.

ISABELLA: I see.

PEPITA: And the CNT comrades started to tell me that I shouldn't have made those declarations. And I replied, "I stand by what I said". I said that, because I was impressed by the way in which that woman came clean about her homosexuality with dignity. And she never made an issue about letting other women do the same. Everyone, including Antonia Fontanilla, told me the same thing, "You shouldn't have said that!" "Listen, I stand by what I said".

ISABELLA: We've watched the video in question together with other women in Barcelona and they were all proud of the courage with which you said such an important thing.

PEPITA: This is precisely what the American woman told me, "No other woman has ever made these declarations". And this is very important, because many lesbians seem to be afraid. I'm not afraid. I don't care if a lesbian pays me a visit at home. It's the same for me and I assert it. One day some French anarchists invited me to Paris for a debate; Mercedes learnt of my arrival; there were also Soledad and other women. So Mercedes Comaposada called me, although it was the first time in many years. She tiptoed around the topic, but I understood what she I meant and said, "Mercedes, do you want to talk to me about the homosexuality of Lucia Sanchez Saornil?"

"Ah," she replied, "Nobody knows if she is or not".

"This is not true! We all know it!" And I added, "We have not seen each other for many years. When we met, I was a girl and you were a woman; I have some wonderful memories of you, but don't forget that my hair has turned white, so we are two women now and we are equals".

When I arrived in Paris, I met Soledad and we took part together in that debate. And I was surprised by her words: for example, she said that we called ourselves free women, but we weren't "free" — this was really annoying.

ISABELLA: What do you mean?

MARTA: I think that you are referring to the fact that you were free but not libertine.

PEPITA: Yes, but this is stupid, isn't it? Did we have to justify ourselves? And even if it were true, who would care? I'll try to make myself clear. We should say what we feel. We wanted that debate to end immediately, because she only justified women. But why should we justify ourselves? When I took the chair, the French comrades were happy, because there were so many people who wanted to participate and speak. And it was true. I don't care for success, but people positively wanted to make things clear. It was amazing. After the debate, Soledad had arranged for a meeting with Mercedes, and I was happy because I had not seen her for many years, but then she told me that Mercedes could not welcome us in her house. I was disappointed and she said, "Let's meet tomorrow in such and such a café," and I replied, "Should I really meet her in a café?" I didn't want to go there. I felt hurt.

Eventually, I gave up and went there, but time passed and she didn't come, so Soledad called and said, "Mercedes wants to talk to you". I didn't want to talk to her, but my friend begged me, "Come Pepita, please come," and Mercedes told me, "I'm sorry, Pepita ..." And I answered, "Mercedes, your age does not justify the contempt that I'm feeling for you". And suddenly she asked me, "Pepita, can you type?" And I replied, "Yes, of course ... why are you asking me that?" And she said, "Do you want to stay a few days with me at my house and be my secretary?" And I answered, "Listen Mercedes, I must take care of my family, my partner, children and grandchildren. Do you really think that I can be your secretary?"

Sara then told me that, when they went to Paris, they were not welcomed by her as well, and I replied, "Do you accept this behaviour?

She can get lost, regardless of the fact that she founded my group". She left a bad taste in my mouth, and I didn't want to hear about her anymore.

MARTA: And what about Suceso Portales?

PEPITA: Ah, she's different. She lived in London and published a magazine. The articles for that magazine were also written by an English friend of ours called Mary Stevenson, who came to our libertarian camp organised by the FIL. The participants came from all over the world, even from Australia.

ISABELLA: Why was Suceso Portales different?

PEPITA: She was a strong woman, one of the strongest women that I've ever met, and this is clear in the video. I was positively impressed by her and told her, "The best speeches in the video are yours". We've never been close, but we became friends when we were shooting the video. We shared the same ideas and I regret having lost touch with her. I'd like to hug her once again.

MARTA: Sara, for example, said that she was a little authoritarian.

PEPITA: I don't think that she was authoritarian; she had her own ideas and put them into practice. Sometimes, when you express your ideas in a frank and clear way, you may make enemies. This often happens. What's your opinion about it?

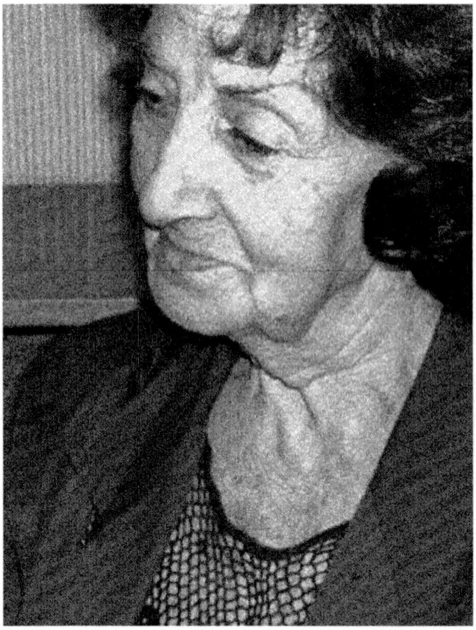

MANOLA RODRIGUEZ
1917-2009
COMMUNIST | Interviewed September 1997, Barcelona

Once whilst in Barcelona for a meeting of feminist groups at the "Ca 'la dona" association, I met Manola and suggested an interview with her. The only Communist (Stalinist) woman among those interviewed that hugged me with the strength of a guerrilla still willing to shoulder a rifle to change the world.

ISABELLA: Hi Manola, how are you?

MANOLA: Well thank you, I'm ready, let's start!

ISABELLA: When did you start dealing with politics and how was your life then?

MANOLA: When I joined the Communist Youth, I was very young; Spain had experienced the dictatorship of Primo de Rivera and the black years, and the workers joined trade unions and associations. My father was arrested before the Republic was proclaimed and I used to pay him visits when I was a child.

ISABELLA: Was he a Communist too?

MANOLA: No, he was an anarchist.

ISABELLA: And what about your mother?

MANOLA: She was an anarchist too, but maybe she was just influenced by my father, because she came from a middle class family. I was the eldest of 12 children of whom four died, and my father took me to the secret meetings of the CNT, which sometimes took place in the countryside or in the basement.

ISABELLA: Was your father the first person who talked to you about politics?

MANOLA: No, because he couldn't study and wasn't able to express his ideas. He was oriented towards action and hated the middle class but wasn't good at dialectics. As a man, he had his own contradictions: at home — he was the master and we had to obey him.

ISABELLA: When did you start working?

MANOLA: I attended a sewing course and started to work as a tailor; there I met a girl, Carmen Torrelo, who talked to me about communism. At that time, I considered myself an anarchist and we spent the afternoons on discussions about politics. I was self-taught and as soon as I had some spare time, I devoted myself to study and politics. I would have liked to study languages and travel to know other countries, but I got married, I had children and focused on other things.

ISABELLA: You were born in Madrid and later moved to Barcelona with your family. Is it right?

MANOLA: Yes, my mother, my brothers and sisters and I moved to Barcelona because my father had some troubles with his political activity. He moved to France and we went to Catalonia. When the Republic was proclaimed in 1931, he was able to return to Spain and we moved back to Madrid; at that time I began to consistently attend Communist meetings.

ISABELLA: How old were you then?

MANOLA: Well ... I was born in 1917, in the year of the revolution, so I was not even 20 years old when the civil war broke out and 15 or 16 when I started to deal with politics.

ISABELLA: At that time did the Communist groups talk about feminism?

MANOLA: Yes, and also about discrimination against women and emancipation; we tried to introduce a feminist model starting from our immediate needs.

ISABELLA: And when did the civil war break out?

MANOLA: In Madrid we were all ready to defend ourselves from a military coup and, when the war broke out, most of us left for the front to fight.

ISABELLA: Did you join them?

MANOLA: Yes, together with some friends of mine. There was little organisation; there was a lack of weapons, food and clothes. But we left anyway to defend the Republic.

ISABELLA: Were there many women on the front?

MANOLA: There were not many, but women fought even in the trenches. Women came from all over the country, from Madrid, from Barcelona, to fight, work in factories and hospitals and fight on the front. I was in the group led by Campesino[1] near Madrid. Initially, we couldn't even shoulder a rifle, we used to shoot randomly. Then the people's army was established, weapons and ammunition were provided, but women were asked to leave the front, because they were needed elsewhere.

ISABELLA: How did you react to this order?

MANOLA: I saw it as a necessity. Women had to take care of civilian life in the country, of children, of the elderly and the sick.

ISABELLA: But many women would have rather stayed on the front and fought.

MANOLA: Those who really wanted to stay managed to remain on the front, but I realised that there were urgent needs to be met. Nobody forced me to leave the front; someone read a circular and explained that it was not appropriate, but rather a real necessity. I was assigned to a hospital where I took care of blood transfusions. In my spare time, I used to prepare my clothes for the front.

ISABELLA: The role played by the Communist Party during the Spanish conflict has been widely debated, assuming that it actually wanted to support a war instead of a revolution.

MANOLA: Yes, the anarchists wanted to make a revolution, especially here in Catalonia. The Communist Party wanted to win the war; only a few wanted a revolution.

ISABELLA: What do you think about it?

---

1. Enrique Lister: A Spanish Communist and military officer.

MANOLA: I think that the time wasn't right for a revolution. The anarchists wanted to take advantage of the situation, but we respected the people's will and the people fought for the Republic.

ISABELLA: What do you think about the repression against the POUM? Do you think that the Communist Party made any mistakes?

MANOLA: There were some political discrepancies between us and them, but I don't regard them as mistakes. The October Revolution (in Russia, 1917) was successful and there were many positive effects here too. The POUM, the Trotskyists, and the anarchists led people to believe that we were enemies. I was a member of the Communist Party, because I believed that we were right, but this doesn't mean that I avoided any contact with the Trotskyists or the anarchists. Some ideas suggested by Trotsky proved to be right, such as, for example, the permanent revolution. He was right from many points of view, but the revolution cannot be improvised.

ISABELLA: With reference to controversial topics, currently, especially after the opening up of the Soviet archives, it was found out that many Spanish and Italian communists, such as Luigi Longo, Palmiro Togliatti and Vittorio Vidali[1], were involved as accomplices or instigators, in many murders of the most revolutionary members of the movement, like Nin, among others. Did this news spread within the movement at that time?

MANOLA: It's always hard to find out what the truth was, but nowadays, based on my experience, I have realised that ideas and theory are not the same thing. At that time, we probably needed to believe in something, therefore we regarded Togliatti or La Pasionaria[2] as legends, without considering their mistakes. But this made us feel part of a bigger movement, it made us feel united and stronger in the fight.

ISABELLA: But Andreu Nin was tortured and killed.

MANOLA: He wasn't killed by me.

ISABELLA: I know, but political responsibility rests with the Communist Party and the PSUC, the Unified Socialist Party of Catalonia. When did the war end?

---
1. Prominent founders of the Italian Communist Party and USSR loyalists.
2. Dolores Ibárruri Gómez, called la Pasionaria (1895-1989) was a Spanish anti-fascist politician. She was president of the PCE, the Communist Party of Spain.

MANOLA: At the time, I had a relationship with a Communist boy, and I got pregnant too. We flew to Valencia and then to Alicante, but the fascists caught us and I gave birth to my first child in a prison cell. An agreement was reached with Franco for the exchange of prisoners; Franco replied, "We won't harm those who are innocent". But this was not true: we were all revolutionaries; actually, they arrested and tortured us.

ISABELLA: Was your partner arrested too?

MANOLA: Yes, and we were separated — we were sent to two different prisons; however, negotiations were made with the enemy. We moved to Alicante because we had been assured that some British ships would rescue us. They told us, "Those who don't want to stay here under Franco's regime should escape". My partner and I knew that they would not respect any agreement, but we had no choice. So we went to Alicante and there the fascists didn't allow the English ships to approach the coast; we saw them in the distance, but we couldn't reach them, and it was a tragedy. We couldn't escape and were arrested! He was sent to a concentration camp and I was imprisoned; we were many, about one thousand, they didn't know what to do with so many people. One day, we were ordered to return home, we were grouped by city and districts. I thought that I had better not say that I was from Madrid, because Madrid had been destroyed, so I stated I came from Valencia, which was the last city to be conquered by the fascists and was less dangerous. In Valencia I had a vague appointment with my partner, "If we are released, we'll meet at the station". We would wait no longer than eight days. Otherwise, we would meet in Almaden in Extremadura, at his parents' house. We wanted to join the guerrilla movement; we couldn't accept the spread of fascism.

In Valencia I saw some women leaving for the cities; they gathered us together as if we were animals along with livestock and goods. I stayed at the station for a fortnight and then travelled to Almadén, to his parents' house. They didn't want to take care of my son and I returned to Madrid. There I hid in a house; later, I learned that the police offered safe-conduct to women and I asked for a safe-conduct pass for both myself and my partner. I forged it and gave it to him when I visited him at the camp.

ISABELLA: Weren't you afraid of being recognised from when you were arrested?

MANOLA: Yes, so I frequently changed my appearance: I put on make-up, bought some hats, some elegant clothes, I tried to look like an upper middle-class woman. My mother took care of my son, but relations with my father had deteriorated. He didn't talk to me anymore, because I was Communist, and he wanted me to leave. As soon as I could, I went to see my partner and one day I was told they would execute him by firing squad. He was a graphic designer and used to make anti-fascist murals. We were constantly escaping death. Desiderio had a forged safe-conduct pass but they were shooting everybody. A man came from Madrid, lined the prisoners up and went, "Yes, no, yes and no ..." and the chosen ones were shot. There was no hope of saving him. But on July 19th 1939 Franco decided on an amnesty! Desiderio was saved and we were so happy when he was released! Later, we were arrested again, but at least we had met up one more time! In Barcelona we hid in the house of some friends of ours and wanted to resume the fight.

ISABELLA: Did you fight against Francoism even during the dictatorship?

MANOLA: Yes, of course, what else could we do? The police went to Desiderio's parents to ask them where he was, and his mother naively said that he was in Barcelona; so they found and arrested him. It was horrible!

ISABELLA: How long was he kept in prison?

MANOLA: For a short time, because in Barcelona there were some lawyers who defended political prisoners and they managed to get them out.

ISABELLA: Let's focus again on machismo and feminism. You told me that you've always been a feminist, but feminism, from a historical point of view, was born and spread throughout America and Europe in the 1970s.

MANOLA: Yes, but in Madrid, during the civil war in the '30s, young Communists like me already talked about the liberation of women; we were aware of the discrimination against women in the political and social sphere and tried to fight against a society which treated us as slaves.

ISABELLA: What can you tell me about Mujeres Libres?

MANOLA: At that time, I used to read the books of Federica Montseny, a former minister for health.

ISABELLA: At that time, the law on abortion was also approved.

MANOLA: Yes, it was an important achievement for women. Obviously, it was abolished during Franco's regime, together with other laws.

ISABELLA: One of the most iconic members of the Communist Party of that time was Dolores Ibárruri, who was called "La Pasionaria".

MANOLA: Yes, she was an extraordinary woman; her oratorical skills were amazing. She had experienced hunger and misery, but finally she redeemed herself thanks to politics. She was a humble and simple woman, but with a great personality. In Madrid there is a foundation dedicated to her which organises debates, conferences and photographic exhibitions; she made our history.

ISABELLA: What are the issues for which Spanish women should fight today?

MANOLA: They should fight for their rights, which are many. It's not true that we no longer live in a patriarchal society as we are led to believe. All over the world, man is the master in his house, although he is oppressed and exploited elsewhere. He has always ruled over "his" woman and women in general. Some comrades of mine wanted to be respected and venerated at home. Women should understand that they should organise a feminist struggle to claim their rights; men will never grant us anything unless we fight. If we are women and revolutionaries, then we must fight twice. Men may even protest on our side in the streets, but we must also fight against them at home.

ISABELLA: Did you meet any lesbians during the civil war or later?

MANOLA: There have always been lesbians. Obviously, today it's more frequent to meet lesbians, because there is more freedom of expression and there are fewer prejudices. When I was young, there were some "strange" women with short hair and very little feminine behaviour. They were called "tortilleras," but they didn't proclaim their sexual choice. As far as I can remember, one of them played an important role within the party, but I never talked to her about certain subjects. Today things are different even here in Barcelona: at Cà la dona I had the opportunity to meet some groups of lesbians.

ISABELLA: What activities have you been involved in recently?

MANOLA: I have joined the Catalan Communist Party; I take care of the female section of a trade union, a Worker Commission and still continue my feminist struggle at Cà la dona, where there are various political groups. I have read a lot of books from the Milan Women's Library, like *Non credere di avere dei diritti*[1], some essay on female authority, and "La fine del patriarcato", which was published in the last issue of *Sottosopra*.

ISABELLA: What do you think about patriarchy?

MANOLA: I think that patriarchy will be eliminated as soon as we really want it. Women often accept the dominant culture and let themselves be influenced by a culture that they would actually like to change somehow.

ISABELLA: But many women cannot choose when and how to change their culture.

MANOLA: This is true; in fact, it's necessary to start from a real class awareness, otherwise we cannot explain many related things, including our real feminist awareness.

ISABELLA: Thank you, Manola.

MANOLA: Thank you. Isabella.

---

1. *Don't Believe You Have Rights*, pub 1987 (Rosenberg & Sellier)

BLANCA NAVARRO

1918-2012
ANARCHIST | Interviewed in Bezier, February 1997

At Radio Contrabanda in Barcelona, I met Marta V. and we hitchhiked to Bezier where we were joined by Sara Berenguer, Rosa Laviña, Dolores Prat, Blanca Navarro (aka Dolores Jiménez Álvarez) and the other women from the Mujeres Libres feminist group. The first interview was with Blanca, who welcomed us on the doorstep after 80 wonderful years of social struggle.

ISABELLA: Hi Blanca, I would like you to tell me about when you started getting involved in politics.

BLANCA: Well, during the civil war I was 18 years old. There were strikes, protests, and demonstrations in the streets.

ISABELLA: Were there also women?

BLANCA: Yes, many women. Many of them left for the front.

ISABELLA: And you joined them didn't you?

BLANCA: Yes, but only later. As soon as the war broke out, I went to the hospital in São Paulo to take care of the injured militants.

ISABELLA: And what did you do when the Civil War began?

BLANCA: I was attending a theatre course, but surprisingly the guys weren't there. Then the sirens sounded announcing the beginning of the revolt and it was chaos. Barricades were built, shots came from every street corner.

ISABELLA: The biggest movement in Catalonia was the anarchist one?

BLANCA: Yes, because the communist movement wasn't well organised. In fact, at that time, the Communist Party had 25,000 members, while Mujeres Libres had 28,000.

ISABELLA: When did you decide to leave for the front?

BLANCA: I stayed in Barcelona until May 1937 then, in August, I got married to Navarro and later decided to leave for the front.

ISABELLA: What happened to you in May 1937?

BLANCA: I tried to recover weapons for my comrades. The government didn't provide the people with weapons since it was more afraid of us than of the fascists. In those days, as happened during the whole revolution, there was a lack of weapons, of food as well as of an efficient organisation. They attacked especially the POUM militants but also us anarchists were persecuted.

The militants were drafted, the collectives were dismantled, their grass-root management was minimised, and women were not allowed to take up arms. They regarded us as traitors, as Francoist supporters — they were crazy. In the summer of 1937 Navarro and I were in Aragon. We had joined the Durruti Column[1] and were about to retreat as required by the central government. Navarro was with those members who were responsible for the organisation and care of secret documents and information. As soon as we met we left, together, for the front.

ISABELLA: What was it like to live on a battlefield?

BLANCA: It was neither easy nor pretty, however it was bearable. I took care of the wounded, tested guns, guarded the weapon warehouse and cooked. The Russian weapons all had to be tested. The government gave us the worst weapons. I shot up in the air and if the guns failed to work properly, then my comrades tried to repair them.

We also looked for means of transport to transport the weapons from one warehouse to another and used trucks to transport the wounded. We walked dozens of miles but I didn't consider that a bad time, perhaps because I was twenty years old and was fascinated by life. Obviously, there was a war, but we were fighting for a just cause. As soon as we stopped, I immediately fell asleep, while my comrades never rested even at night.

ISABELLA: After May 1937, the government ordered women to retreat from the front.

BLANCA: Yes, because we were accused of infecting the soldiers would you believe? But I refused to leave the front and kept on fighting in the trenches.

---

1. The largest single anarchist force during the war, comprising more than 6,000 fighters.

ISABELLA: There were just a few women on the front, weren't there?

BLANCA: Yes, we were few and hindered in many ways.

ISABELLA: Do you think that there was sexism among your comrades?

BLANCA: Yes and no. They tried to behave as best they could, but they were conditioned by the surrounding situation. Actually, I felt protected rather than discriminated against.

ISABELLA: What do you mean?

BLANCA: For example, there wasn't much food but I was deprived of nothing.

ISABELLA: On the front were you treated like Blanca or like Navarro's partner?

BLANCA: I wasn't somebody's partner, I was simply Blanca. Actually, Blanca was my nom de guerre — my real name is Dolores. In spite of the horror of the times I was lucky, because I was able to share a dramatic experience with extraordinary people. For example, the fascists bombarded us while we were on a truck so we had to protect ourselves to survive. It was horrible.

ISABELLA: When women were on the front, did they have access to abortion or contraception?

BLANCA: When a militant got pregnant, she left the front and returned to the city. Sometimes they joined us again after the child was born. Sometimes they didn't. It depended on each individual case.

ISABELLA: In December 1936 a law on the liberalisation of abortion was passed in Catalonia and it was a great achievement for women all over the world.

BLANCA: Yes, it was a great step forward, however, women never needed a law to abort. Obviously, a law which granted the right to abortion was a great achievement for the women's movement, a great recognition of our social and political role. Women weren't just baby factories, but were also militants, soldiers, rebels, fighters.

ISABELLA: Can you tell me something about the women who created the Mujeres Libres movement? Do you know any of them?

BLANCA: Mujeres Libres was a political group of women which was established before the civil war and at its peak it brought together about thirty thousand women across Republican Spain. They were very brave and skilful. The core was based in Madrid but it was spread throughout Catalonia. Most of them previously belonged to the anarchist movement while others had no past political experience. Many of them became anarchists after having got in touch with Mujeres Libres. However, as a political organisation, it was closely linked to the CNT[1], the FAI[2], the SIA[3], as well as to the anarchist movement. I personally knew some of them, while others only by name.

ISABELLA: You never wanted to join a group made up only of women?

BLANCA: No, the "Mujeres Libres" group was very important in that period, but I decided to join mixed groups and to share my personal choices with men as well. I've always wanted to join forces with men.

ISABELLA: What happened to you after the end of the civil war?

BLANCA: On February 7th 1939 we reached the French border. Partly on foot, partly with a truck belonging to the International Solidarity group. I stayed in a small village on the border for five or six days where I hid weapons inside some aluminium barrels, but the worst thing was, we didn't know whether the French would welcome us or not. On one side, the Francoists kept on bombing us, while, on the other end, the negotiations with the French authorities were extremely slow. We were hungry, overwhelmed by pain and discomfort. We had lost a war that we should have won, we walked barefoot and desperate, in search of shelter from the enemy's bombs.

---

1. Confederaction Nacional del Trabajo. (National Confederation of Labour) Anarchist organisation founded in 1910 in Barcelona, which played a key role during the 1936-39 Spanish Revolution.
2. Federación Anarquista Ibérica (Iberian Anarchist Federation). The FAI was founded in 1927 to preserve the anarchist orientation of the CNT and prevent the organisation from losing its ability to represent the working class.
3. Solidarité Internationale Antifasciste. (International Anti-Fascist Solidarity). An organisation which arranged for solidarity during the Spanish revolution and then welcomed and protected the political refugees.

ISABELLA: How were you finally welcomed then?

BLANCA: It was a terrible experience — we had to leave our belongings at the border. Fortunately, I had just the bare essentials, very little money, and a plain bracelet. At the money exchange office, they gave me 17 francs. What could I ever do with that small amount of money in a foreign country!

ISABELLA: What happened then?

BLANCA: They separated men from women and children. We arrived in Le Puy, which is a horrible place, full of churches and convents like Lourdes or Burgos. As soon as the train stopped someone told us that we would be safe because there wouldn't be any bombing there. Women were welcomed by a delegation from the Prefecture as well as by the Ecclesiastical Authorities. We stayed in a sort of convent for one night then, the following morning, we reached a village where we were hosted in a nursing home. We spent eleven months surrounded by religious women who forced us to go to mass every week.

Before Easter, they sent us a priest for confession. We said that we didn't speak French but they "reassured" us that he was Spanish. That priest had a paternalistic approach. He regarded us as war victims. When we told him that we had fought for a just cause, he railed at us because "women like us" had set fire to churches and killed religious people. We answered that anyone who sided with the fascists was our enemy, regardless of their religious status. Then he talked about fraternal love and we asked him if we could see our comrades. He answered that we were "asking too much" and then the conflict between us broke out openly. He was a young priest and we remembered him well, because, from that day on, the nuns stopped giving us sweets on Sunday mornings, "You behaved badly with him and he didn't deserve this treatment". Well, we didn't care. May he rest in peace!

ISABELLA: It was such a cruelty.

BLANCA: Yes, especially because I liked sweets.

ISABELLA: What did you do then?

BLANCA: To save money, when we wrote to our comrades, we put soap on stamps and reused them several times. One day, we went into a bakery, where there was the wife of a socialist councillor, we told her about the priest. She was shocked and after that she bought us sweets every Sunday!

After some months, the French and the Spanish governments entered into negotiations. Franco said that anyone who had not committed acts of violence would be allowed to return to Spain. Obviously, forgiveness would be granted especially to women and children. The municipality sent delegates to get us to sign the necessary documentation to ask the Spanish government to readmit us into the country, but we didn't want to sign any document without first asking the opinion of our comrades. We knew that Franco would imprison and execute them! We weren't revolutionaries for nothing! Meanwhile, they kept on sending us delegates from the municipality: socialists, communists, republicans, but we didn't sign any document. We were so resolute. In the other camps, many women decided to return to Spain but, as soon as they arrived in Perpignan, they were shocked by the atrocities of Francoism and came back to France.

ISABELLA: How long did you stay there?

BLANCA: I was one of the first who left, in December 1939, and finally met my partner on January 2nd 1940 in Cordes.

ISABELLA: So did you decide to stay in France or arrange to come back to Spain?

BLANCA: We decided to stay in France, because in Spain Franco had executed half of the anti-fascists and had imprisoned the other half. We wouldn't survive under such a regime.

ISABELLA: Did you continue your political activity here in France?

BLANCA: Yes, of course. We never stopped. In Cordes we received many people as guests. We arranged a small health facility and even revived our political organisation. On Sundays, together with other women we used to ride our bicycle from Cordes to another town to help with the sick at the hospital and bring them some food. These may seem small things, but, in times of war, with so much misery and hunger, everything becomes even bigger. Our group of women also held literacy and theatre courses.

PILAR: What happened when the city was invaded by the Nazis?

BLANCA: Obviously we were persecuted and had to hide. I also had to burn my partner's letters from the concentration camp. I had French documentation, but Navarro was taken to a German labour camp. They had to repair German warships. It was horrible because they were forced to spend the whole day in the water with severe health risks. One day, he came home with a special licence that we could forge, and he managed to escape. We had French and German documentation, but I didn't speak French and he didn't speak German. What a pair! When we were stopped by the Germans, we showed them our French documents and vice versa when stopped by the French. That is how we survived until the end of the Second World War.

PILAR: Did you participate in any specific resistance action?

BLANCA: We never took part in actions alongside the armed groups of the resistance, but we hid several people and helped others to escape. One day we hid a biker in our house and forgot his helmet on the table. This proves how our lives depended on small details.

ISABELLA: But how was it possible to hide yourselves from the Nazis?

BLANCA: We soon realised that we were supported by the town mayor. When we needed something, he was always ready to help us. Initially, we believed that he was simply a nice person. Then we found out that he was an anti-fascist militant. For some time, we hosted a family of six or seven people in our house and the mayor, Monsieur Morel, congratulated us.

ISABELLA: You were telling me about your imprisonment.

BLANCA: Yes. That was in 1946. At that time Navarro was in prison in Barcelona, because he had planned an attack against Franco together with other anarchists. I was sent by the organisation to get in contact with the militants of Barcelona to coordinate underground activities. I arrived there on December 9th 1946 and returned to Toulouse on January 7th 1947. When I tried to cross the French border, I was arrested but only for a couple of days. Well, that's enough for now, maybe we can meet again in a few days, if it's OK for you.

ISABELLA: Yes, of course Blanca, see you soon! Have a nice day.

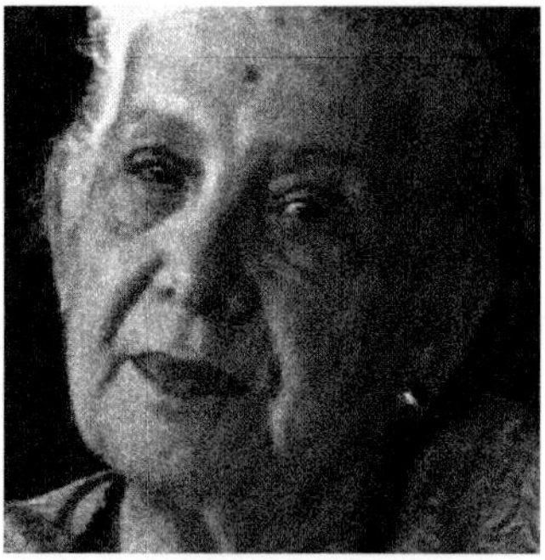

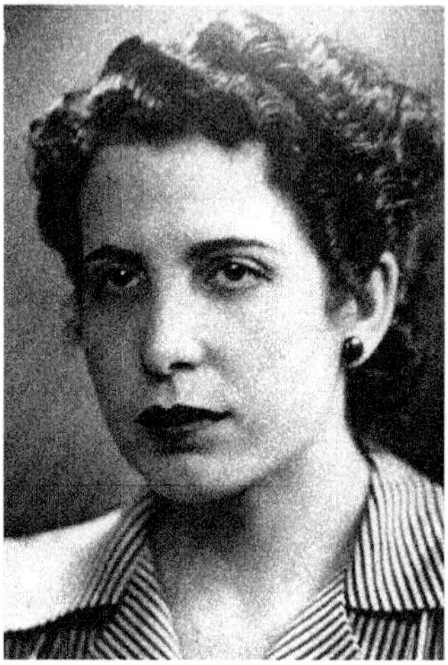

SUCESO PORTALES
(1904-1999)
ANARCHIST | Interviewed September 1997, Madrid

In 1997 I moved to Madrid and tried to get in contact with Suceso, one of the founders of Mujeres Libres. I didn't imagine that she could still be alive and would want to talk to me about her life. When I knocked on her door, Ortensia opened the door and ushered me in to see her friendly grandmother, who was waiting for me.

ISABELLA: Hello Suceso, I would like to know something about the group Mujeres Libres. How and when was it established? Who founded it?

SUCESO: Mujeres Libres was an anarchist political organisation which was set up in Spain in April 1936, some months before the beginning of the Civil War. It was established by Lucía Sánchez Saornil, Mercedes Comaposada and Amparo Poch y Gascón. The group numbered about 20,000 women during the war, who mostly came from humble cultural and social backgrounds. We were so proud of the fact that so many women decided to fight against the prejudices of their husbands, fathers and brothers by joining our group; they were simple women, who could barely read and write their names.

ISABELLA: Why did you become a member of this political organisation?

SUCESO: Because it was an organisation of anarchist women and enriched my political development. I had always been a member of libertarian groups, but there was no real debate about the condition of women within the anarchist groups. My comrades benefited and still benefit from a patriarchal culture that has always considered men to be the agents of history. Women had to organise themselves, fighting inside and outside their homes, inside and outside the party premises. We wanted to use our energy to participate more extensively in the political life of our country, but our comrades hindered us, so we decided to change our lives before trying to change the world.

ISABELLA: What was your political experience?

SUCESO: I came from an anarchist family from Guadalajara. My father was a teacher and my aunt, Remedio Portales, created an anarchist group in Badajoz. We were self-taught and used to read Bakunin, Proudhon, and Malatesta[1].

ISABELLA: Did women participate in political life?

SUCESO: No, of course not. Women cut themselves out of politics or politics cut them out, I don't know.

ISABELLA: Why did you decide to join a group of women?

SUCESO: Because we needed to organise ourselves independently and fight for our condition. I met Lucía Sáchez Saornil, Amparo Poch and Mercedes Comaposada and was impressed by their struggle.

ISABELLA: Had you already met them before joining Mujeres Libres?

SUCESO: No, I met them when I became a member of the feminist group. I was born in a small village in the provinces; I had read many books, but had never actively participated in any group of women simply because there were no women's groups in my village. I was one of the first who joined Mujeres Libres. I felt the strength and need to be part of a group of women only. The libertarian youth didn't care about the condition of women; male comrades didn't share political news, they left "their" women at home to look after their children. So we needed to claim our struggle.

ISABELLA: What were the main activities of Mujeres Libres?

SUCESO: We mainly dealt with the women's literacy; many of them couldn't even read or write and thus couldn't take part in the social life of the country.

---

1. Mikhail Bakunin (1814-76) and Pierre Joseph Proudhon (1809-65) were two of anarchism's most famous early philosophers. The former clashed with Marx in the First International, while Proudhon was the first prominent French figure to declare himself an anarchist in the modern sense, publishing the seminal *What is Property?* in 1840. Errico Malatesta (1853-1932) was probably the most influential anarchist of the late 19th and early 20th centuries, involved in revolutionary activities all over Europe.

ISABELLA: Were you in contact with other republican feminist groups, for example with Communist women?

SUCESO: We had limited contact with them because politics divided us. Our common goal was women's emancipation, but the Communist women depended too much on their party politics. Their organisation was efficient from a political point of view. Spanish women were deeply influenced by Catholic culture and were afraid of joining radical anarchist organisations. We criticised the power of the Church which wanted to hush up women's claims.

ISABELLA: How were your relations with your male comrades?

SUCESO: It may sound strange, but many comrades, including the anarchists, not only didn't support us, but even hindered our political activity. They couldn't understand why we organised meetings for women only. They believed that we were going to split up the anarchist movement, that we didn't know who our "real" enemy was; they tried to teach us how to be involved in politics at a given moment in time but we were interested in building the future. This was absurd; probably the same thing is happening right now.

ISABELLA: Yes, exactly.

SUCESO: From a political point of view, they supported, financed and helped us when we had conflicts with other organisations, but they didn't understand the reasons for our struggle; evidently, we represented the contradiction of their cultural limits.

ISABELLA: How were your relations with the other women in the organisation?

SUCESO: I had good, sincere, and friendly relations with the other members of Mujeres Libres as well as with the other women of the radical left wing. Obviously, we had some problems with middle-class women; most of them were Francoists and, as soon as the war broke out, they followed their class interests instead of the gender ones. Middle-class women may be subjugated by their husbands at home and, at the same time, may legitimate the abuses perpetrated by the ruling class to which they belong. We were looking for women willing to fight inside and outside their house. Therefore, they should learn how to read and write in order to become autonomous and independent, free and rebellious. We had to fight against everything and everyone, and especially against the Catholic tradition that required silence and resignation from women.

ISABELLA: Your daughter Ortensia told me that you were one of the first women who drove a car.

SUCESO: Yes, it's true: we set ourselves so many goals; we wanted to be free and independent, strong and courageous. Driving cars, trucks, buses was a necessity, a political and cultural redemption for us, especially with respect to middle-class women who didn't need to work.

ISABELLA: In France and Spain I met other women who joined Mujeres Libres, like Pepita Carpena and Sara Guillem, and I asked them if they regarded themselves as feminists and they said no.

SUCESO: You know, maybe today things are different, but, at that time, only middle-class women defined themselves as feminists. They aimed at power, fought for suffrage and the right to vote, while anarchists rejected power and were abstentionists. We didn't care about elections. We used to fight along the streets, in the houses, in the squares. We rejected power games which distracted people from active politics, that's why we regarded ourselves as "feminine" instead of "feminist".

ISABELLA: Moreover, feminism spread in Europe and in the United States in the '70s and was characterised by class awareness and the criticism of capitalist and patriarchal society. Therefore, it's not a middle-class movement, but rather a mass, proletarian movement which opposes the system. Were there discussions on lesbianism at that time? Lucia, one of the founders of Mujeres Libres, had a love affair for years with another woman ...

SUCESO: That's not true! I was one of her closest friends and Lucia never crossed the "limits" of decency!

ISABELLA: Pepita Carpena said that Lucia had love affairs with women.

SUCESO: No, it's not true.

ISABELLA: Whatever the truth, I'm not scandalised.

SUCESO: Yes, of course, there would be nothing wrong with that, but Lucia was not that kind of woman. However, these are private issues. Lucia was nice, she was the intellectual of the group. Her father worked for the public administration and had offered Lucia the opportunity to study. Lucia was smart, perspicacious; she worked in the field of data processing, which was as important as lawyers today; then she became interested in anarchism and the CNT.

ISABELLA: Can we consider Lucia the most "political" member of the group?

SUCESO: No, Lucia was more "intellectual" than political in the sense that the word is used today. At that time, it was very hard for women to be in politics; women were subjugated by the Catholic Church. My father's mother, for example, was the maid of the most Catholic woman in the country, but my aunt, Rimedio Portales, was one of the first women who founded an anarchist group. I couldn't study; my father was a teacher and earned little money. My elder sister was able to continue her studies, unlike me. My father earned 5,400 pesetas a year and had six children; my mother got pregnant 14 times.

ISABELLA: Basically she got pregnant almost every year!

SUCESO: Yes, my mother was an extraordinary woman. She had a Catholic, apostolic, Roman education, but was a wonderful, open-minded and sympathetic mother. She came from a humble family and wasn't able to study, but she gave us a good education and didn't deprive us of anything.

ISABELLA: Were there many women who decided to fight on the front?

SUCESO: Yes, but the members of Mujeres Libres thought that women should rather learn how to read and write instead of shouldering a rifle. We stood in the rear. We focused on more radical activities to be carried out in the houses and in society. When the war broke out, many women decided to fight, but then an organised army was sent to the front and women started to deal with other things.

ISABELLA: Mujeres Libres also took care of sexuality, contraception.

SUCESO: At that time contraception were considered to be on a par with pornography. This is the reason why women had so many children: because they couldn't prevent pregnancies.

ISABELLA: When did you get married?

SUCESO: I got married to Roman during the civil war. His father was a soldier and his family was Catholic. He was a good boy, but one day he disappeared and I had no idea what happened to him; then I got married to an Andalusian anarchist boy, Acacio, and we had a daughter.

ISABELLA: When did your struggle end?

SUCESO: I left the country with the last train of the CNT heading to Paris. France was full of Spanish refugees and didn't know what to do with us. In Paris, we got stuck on the train for six to seven hours; we had no legal or political status. On one side there was Franco, on the other side there were the Nazis. The situation was uncertain and France tried to protect itself. Then the British government welcomed us as refugees, so we moved to London. I remember the last night that I spent in Spain: I was on a beach along the coast of Valencia (at that time the Spanish government had moved to Valencia) and I thought that we had lost the war, and that therefore we would have to leave our dear country. Mujeres Libres also held its meetings in Valencia. Lucia was the secretary of the organisation and I was the deputy secretary. Our books and documentation all got lost.

ISABELLA: How did the political activity of Mujeres Libres actually start at local level?

SUCESO: As soon as we arrived in a town, we organised a debate on the condition of women. As I already said, Spanish women, at that time, were culturally oppressed by the Catholic Church. They spent most of their leisure time in activities related to the Catholic Church, however, when we talked about their conditions, they answered that prayers would not help them improve their lives. Therefore, many of them joined Mujeres Libres and began to fight against many prejudices. They were very courageous, considering the context. The only thing that they knew was the catechism; they often couldn't read or write.

ISABELLA: Was your organisation supported by your comrades?

SUCESO: Many of them supported us, also from a political point of view, but didn't understand our political activity. They argued that if an anarchist society was intended to set everyone free, then it should also set women free; they didn't realise that the education of women was completely different from theirs, they didn't understand that we were fighting also against them. Later, they noticed that many women were interested in their political activity, thus they grasped the limitations of male "single thought" which ruled the political sphere of that time. They feared that we would deprive them of their privileges, and they were not totally wrong. If there hadn't been so much machismo even within the same left-wing organisations, Mujeres Libres wouldn't have been created.

ISABELLA: What was the political structure of Mujeres Libres?

SUCESO: Each group enjoyed total freedom and independence, but there was a national committee which met regularly in Valencia to plan the political activity of the group. The organisation relied on provincial and regional committees; there were congresses and meetings. We were a solid and well-knit group, and we were proud of our activity, because we were fighting not only against fascism and class prejudice, but also against the prevailing machismo, even that of our partners and comrades.

ISABELLA: How was your life in London?

SUCESO: It was not easy but very happy. It's not easy to live in exile: you miss your culture, your people and even your language, but we didn't stop our activity and wrote articles for a newspaper under the name Mujeres Libres. However, after our exile, we lost contact with one another. Franco's coup ruined our life.

ISABELLA: If you could turn back time, is there anything that you wouldn't do?

SUCESO: I would do exactly what I did. I paid the price for my ideas, for having founded a group of women in reactionary and fascist Spain; it wasn't easy to tilt at windmills, live in exile, return home and struggle every day, but, after all, I was a lucky woman. I have always done what I wanted to, being proud of having struggled to improve the condition of many women in my country. Now life is easier for you today, but at that time there was no education, no freedom. We couldn't vote, raise our voice, sing, or freely walk along the streets. So we created a group of women and a newspaper. Nowadays, youth just wants to have fun, but politics was extremely important to us. I hope that I've made myself clear.

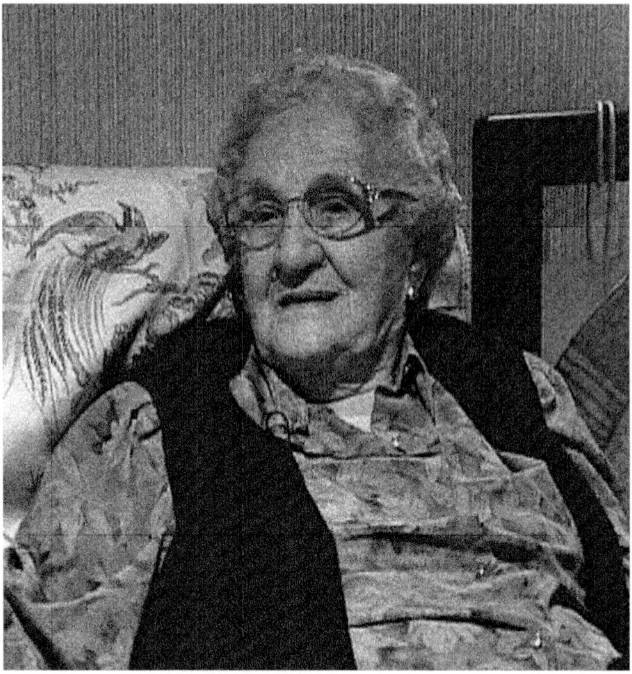

TERESA CARBÓ

(1908-2010)
POUM | Interviewed June 2010, France

In Barcelona, I had bumped into Teresa several times, but I was surprised and excited by the fact that she was still alive and 102 years old. Marta and I decided to visit her in France and talk to her about one of the most important issues in her life: her meeting with Nin in the Stalinist prisons. The Communists tortured her, but she never felt sorry for anything and never changed her version of the events; she is a great example for those who don't sell out to the enemy.

MARTA: Hello Teresa, this is Isabella. She wants to talk to you about the POUM.

TERESA: How did you get here?

ISABELLA: Your niece Silvia gave us your address; we told her that we would come here to have an interview with another woman of the POUM and hoped that we could talk to you too.

TERESA: Who is this other woman of the POUM?

ISABELLA: Teresa Rebull, who lives near Perpignan. Teresa, I don't know if you remember me, but we've already met in Barcelona with the other POUM militants.

TERESA: Are you a journalist?

ISABELLA: No, I'm a historian and I'm writing an essay on Nin. Can you tell me something about the moment when you met him in prison?

TERESA: Nin was killed by the Communists; I met him in a Stalinist prison.

ISABELLA: Do you remember what he told you and how the meeting was?

TERESA: I went to the prison because I had joined Socorro Rojo[1] and took care of the prisoners; as soon as I saw him, I approached him.

ISABELLA: Were you a nurse?

TERESA: Yes, I was a nurse.

ISABELLA: When you saw Nin, did you already know that he had been arrested?

TERESA: I was looking for him precisely because they told me that they had arrested him. When he saw me, he said, "What are you doing here, you fool?" He knew that it was dangerous.

ISABELLA: And then?

TERESA: I was arrested and tortured because I talked to him.

ISABELLA: People were protesting after the disappearance of Nin.

TERESA: He was killed in Alcalá de Henarez.

ISABELLA: Did you stay in Barcelona after the war?

TERESA: I stayed in Barcelona until 1940, then we left and returned there some years later.

ISABELLA: You lived in France and in Latin America, is that right?

TERESA: Yes.

ISABELLA: In which town of Latin America?

TERESA: In Santa Cruz de la Sierra, in Bolivia.

ISABELLA: Why did you go so far away?

---

1. Red Aid — a social service organisation set up as an alternative to the Communist fronted International Red Aid

TERESA: After the war, we went to France, but my son wanted to live in Bolivia, while my partner and I preferred Mexico.

ISABELLA: Most POUM militants went there, like Victor Alba, Pilar Santiago ...

TERESA: Pilar Santiago died suddenly. We were close friends; she visited me in Palafrugell, we wanted to spend some time together.

ISABELLA: She was a wonderful woman. She spent many years in Mexico; she liked art, painting and many other things. When you were arrested after talking to Nin, did you meet any other important people in prison?

TERESA: Maria Teresa Andrade[1], Pilar Santiago ...

ISABELLA: Did you come back to Barcelona after Franco's death?

TERESA: I returned there in 1968. I followed my husband. Then we moved to Palafrugell, so I could often visit my mother.

ISABELLA: Had you also met other members of the POUM? Have you known Teresa Rebull for a long time?

TERESA: Yes, I've known her for a long time.

ISABELLA: And did she live in Barcelona?

TERESA: Yes, her husband Pepe was very famous: he was a member of the party and had been imprisoned even before the war.

ISABELLA: So you lived between Barcelona, Palafrugell, and France?

TERESA: I spent a little time in Spain after the war, then we moved to France, because my husband worked as a decorator. First to Toulouse and then to Paris.

ISABELLA: Why did you join the POUM as a young girl? Why did you choose specifically this party?

---

1. Andrade was a journalist and founded POUM's Women's Secretariat. She was arrested in the 1937 repression and after the war was exiled to Paris.

TERESA: Because we wanted to unify the socialist parties; our party was Marxist, and we wanted to unify the left wing.

ISABELLA: Besides Nin, did you know Maurín?[1]

TERESA: I didn't know Maurín well, because, when the war broke out, he remained in the area occupied by the fascists and was arrested.

ISABELLA: What was Nin like?

TERESA: He was kind and intelligent.

ISABELLA: Were you proud of being a member of this party?

TERESA: Yes, because we wanted to unify the left-wing parties, that is precisely what is being done today. And what's your job?

ISABELLA: I live in Italy and I'm a historian. I came here after the publication of a book on the POUM and the murder of Nin. You are the only one who saw him alive in a Stalinist prison. After the events occurred in May, the newspaper was closed, many escaped, there was a trial, it was a hard moment. Teresa, what do you think about Dolores Ibarruri, La Pasionaria?

TERESA: La Pasionaria was a member of the Communist Party and we had nothing to do with them.

ISABELLA: And what about Federica Montseny?

TERESA: Federica Montseny supported us during the trial. The Stalinists were fanatical. One day one of them pointed a gun at me only to frighten me. "Shoot, if you dare!" I told him.

ISABELLA: Where did that happen?

TERESA: In Barcelona, during the trial; he pointed the gun at my hips.

ISABELLA: Did you attend the trial?

---

1. Joaquín Maurín Juliá was a Spanish politician, communist activist and the leader of the BOC.

TERESA: Yes, I was there.

ISABELLA: Were you a witness or just a spectator?

TERESA: I went to see my comrades; we slept on the street to reserve a place, they didn't want us to be there. Three or four us went there and documented what happened; it's a long story.

ISABELLA: Your testimony is important.

TERESA: I could write a book to tell my story.

ISABELLA: Surely! Everyone regards you as a strong woman, who never changed her opinion about the POUM and Nin in spite of the price paid.

TERESA: I don't feel sorry for anything, because I did nothing wrong; we were deprived of everything, especially from an emotional point of view.

ISABELLA: Was your husband a POUM militant too?

TERESA: Yes.

ISABELLA: What was his name?

TERESA: Esteban Model.

ISABELLA: How many children have you got, Teresa?

TERESA: Two; they live in France. I'm glad that the repression is over, but I don't feel sorry for anything, I didn't hurt anyone.

ISABELLA: Had you been to Brazil too?

TERESA: Yes, from Santa Cruz de la Sierra, in Bolivia, where we lived for seven years, we went to Brazil, to Sao Paulo, and then back to Europe.

ISABELLA: Teresa, if Nin's granddaughters were here, what would you tell them?

TERESA: I would tell them that their grandfather was the best and the most intelligent man in the world. What are the names of Nin's granddaughters?

ISABELLA: Silvia and Cristina; they never met their grandfather.

TERESA: Please, tell them that he was a great person.

ISABELLA: I'll tell them. Can we take a picture together?

TERESA: It's not worth it.

ISABELLA: We may take a picture only of your face.

TERESA: Do whatever you want, I'm still fit.

MARTA: We would like to be 100 old and look like you!

TERESA: My granddaughter lives in Palafrugell and is a journalist. Ah ... I lost my memory and I have some eye problem. I'm sorry if my memory fails.

MARTA: Have you got any brothers or sisters?

TERESA: I had one brother and two sisters, Paquita and Elvira.

MARTA: I met Paquita.

TERESA: Yes ... I was telling you that the POUM protested against injustices. Under Franco, no-one protested anymore; I stood alone for six months.

ISABELLA: I watched the *The Nikolai Case* film: your testimony is very important. I met Solano, Rocabert. I'm going to meet Elvira Godás this week and I have an appointment with Teresa Rebull in a few hours.

TERESA: She wrote a book; I've not seen her for a long time, I thought she was dead.

ISABELLA: No, she's fine. She was also a singer, wasn't she?

TERESA: Yes, she had a beautiful voice. Tell her I'm happy to know that she's well. I'm sorry if I argued with her or hurt her on some occasions.

ISABELLA: OK, I'll tell her. You are a very combative woman and I still remember the first time I saw you. I immediately understood that you were combative.

TERESA: And I'm still combative, Je ne regrette rien. Many things have happened.

ISABELLA: You'll have more to tell when we see you again.

TERESA: Do you know that I studied Esperanto? I am an Esperantist.

MARTA: And do you remember any Esperanto words?

TERESA: Yes, I remember some.

MARTA: Did you meet Rosa Laviña in Toulouse?

TERESA: Yes, Rosa was an anarchist.

MARTA: And did you often meet?

TERESA: Yes, but you ... what do you think about this?

MARTA: Your generation is so inspiring for us, thanks to what you did and left us. I would like to come back here and have another interview with you.

TERESA: Yes, but I'm slipping every day.

ISABELLA: Actually, looking at you, I wouldn't think so.

TERESA: I'm not sorry for anything, because nobody can say that I was wrong. They deprived us of everything and left us in misery.

MARTA: Why were you tortured in prison?

TERESA: It is what it is. After all, we were imprisoned.

ISABELLA: Why did you join the party? There were also anarchist or other groups at that time.

TERESA: Yes, there were many groups, but we were the Workers' Party of Marxist Unification.

ISABELLA: Have you always been aware of your Marxist orientation?

TERESA: Yes.

ISABELLA: And why did you move to Barcelona?

TERESA: I moved there with my husband, but first we got married in Palafrugell, we opted for the civil ceremony.

ISABELLA: And did you have trouble with your family for this decision?

TERESA: No, when I met my husband, I was already studying Esperanto.

MARTA: And who encouraged you to study Esperanto?

TERESA: We attended a lesson and a teacher explained the grammatical rules, the definition of names and pronouns. It's a language like any other, so I wanted to study it. We met in Malavellas, where there was a mineral water factory. I was seventeen years old and my husband was seven years older than me. I started dating him, because he was more intelligent than me: he used to correct my mistakes when I wrote, and this is how our relationship began. Then we joined the POUM almost at the same time.

ISABELLA: When did you get married?

TERESA: In 1928. My first child was born in 1930. I'm just 20 years older than him.

MARTA: Do you remember the Universal Exposition?

TERESA: Yes, I remember it well.

MARTA: That was the origin of the labour movement ...

TERESA: No, the labour movement has always existed. Maybe, the anarchist movement preceded the Universal Exposition[1].

ISABELLA: Teresa, do you regard yourself as a feminist? Do you believe in the need for a struggle of women only?

---

1. The Universal Exposition of Barcelona was held between 1929 and 1939. In Barcelona there had already been a universal exposition in 1888, which drove the economy of the city. Therefore, a new exposition was arranged to increase the popularity of Catalonia abroad.

TERESA: There should be no difference between men and women, we are all the same.

ISABELLA: Did you work in Bolivia?

TERESA: I've always worked, but in Santa Cruz I did what I could.

MARTA: Were you in contact with people from other organisations or with other people in exile?

TERESA: Yes, we had a lot of friends. One of them was Salvator Ric, who was called the revolutionary socialist.

ISABELLA: Was he also a member of the POUM?

TERESA: No, he was a socialist.

ISABELLA: So now we are somewhere in Europe, between Italy, France and Spain.

TERESA: What does Italy have to do with it?

ISABELLA: I'm Italian, Teresa. Were you a Workers and Peasants Bloc (BOC) militant before joining the POUM?

TERESA: Yes, I was a militant of the BOC of Maurín.

ISABELLA: OK, Teresa. That's all! Thank you for helpfulness.

TERESA: Thank you ... girls ... I can't remember your names. ...

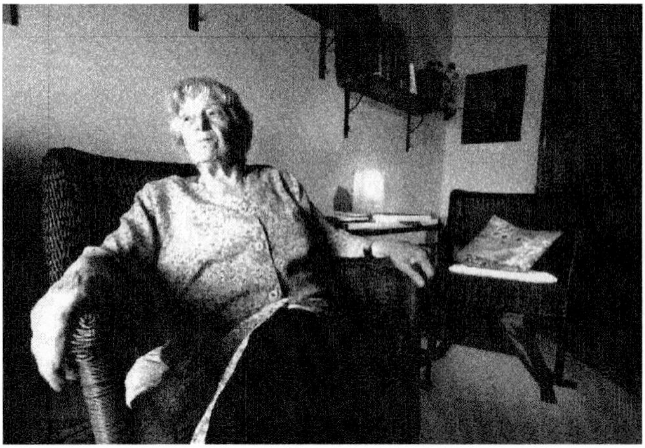

CONCHA PEREZ

1915-2014
Anarchist | Interviewed December 2010, Barcelona

Once back in Barcelona, I met Concha in a nursing home near the sea. She was called "Concha the anarchist" by the journalists from all over the world. That time she wanted me to tell her something about the Italian libertarian movement, so I told her about Berneri, Mara Cagol and Sacco and Vanzetti[1]; she smiled with satisfaction and urged me to start the interview.

ISABELLA: Well Concha, now let's talk about you. Do you like this nursing home?

CONCHA: They treat me very well, I can't complain.

ISABELLA: Good! Now I would like you to tell me something about the political climate during the revolution.

CONCHA: At that time, we talked about anarchism and communism, we discussed everything.

ISABELLA: What was the difference between the anarchist and the Communist movement?

CONCHA: The communists were governed by a central committee, a dictatorship, while we were fighting for freedom.

ISABELLA: When the civil war broke out, what were you doing?

CONCHA: I was already an anarchist militant, but we were forced to take on a military attitude. We turned civil factories into military ones and had to work hard.

---

1. Cagol was a member of the Red Brigades in the early 1970s. She was killed in a shootout with police in 1975. Sacco and Vanzetti were anarchists whose execution in the US after a heavily biased trial in 1921 became a global scandal.

ISABELLA: What products were manufactured?

CONCHA: We manufactured bullets. The owner gave up the factory and production continued even without her. We planned our shifts, although we preferred working during the day, because the size of the bullets had to be extremely precise.

ISABELLA: So were you working at the factory when the war broke out?

CONCHA: Before the war, 12 or 15 people worked there, and then we were almost 100. There was also a nursery school for children. We used to work very hard.

ISABELLA: Can you tell us anything about your private life at that time? Did you have a partner?

CONCHA: At that time, I had a partner and, as soon as the war broke out, we left together for the front.

ISABELLA: Could women fight in trenches?

CONCHA: I left for the front with some women, but most of them cooked, washed clothes and took care of the sick. I hadn't gone there to help anyone; I had gone there to fight.

ISABELLA: Could you shoot?

CONCHA: Yes, obviously! We attacked at night and kept a close watch on the surrounding area during the day. One day, my partner was injured, he had several bullet shards in his arm, and I had to stop the bleeding. His testicle was injured too and I called the Red Cross; it was tragic, because he suffered very much.

ISABELLA: How was the militia organised?

CONCHA: We managed it on our own.

ISABELLA: Were there any other girls?

CONCHA: Yes, but only some of them shouldered a rifle.

ISABELLA: But you were a member of the militia.

CONCHA: Yes, there were also other girls who were part of the militia.

ISABELLA: What was your daily life like? I mean the food, the clothes, the military activities.

CONCHA: We used to visit the villages, stay with the people, and arrange for everything with their help.

ISABELLA: How many of you were there?

CONCHA: We were in groups of ten or 12, and all in all we were 100. We watched over the territory to avoid being taken by surprise by the enemy, waiting for the order to attack. But we lacked weapons and ammunition and were afraid of starting an attack and running out of ammunition.

ISABELLA: Was it hard to become a member of the militia?

CONCHA: For me, it was a natural thing, because I was surrounded by friends of mine and there, in the trenches, even my relationship became stronger. When we went to Barcelona on leave, our comrades lent us a small apartment. After all, we needed some privacy.

ISABELLA: What was your partner's name?

CONCHA: Ramón Robles.

ISABELLA: Did you stay there until the end of the civil war?

CONCHA: No, we returned to Barcelona before the end of the war.

ISABELLA: Did this happen because Durruti ordered women to withdraw from the front?

CONCHA: Durruti gave this order but I didn't obey him and kept on fighting; we couldn't leave the front during the civil war!

ISABELLA: So do you think that that order amounted to discrimination against women?

CONCHA: Yes! Women were fighting just like men, perhaps even harder.

ISABELLA: Had you ever felt discriminated against as a woman on the front?

CONCHA: No, they respected us; there was no abuse, never.

ISABELLA: During the civil war there was the Stalinist repression after the events in May.

CONCHA: We were away from the fighting; we were all united on the front.

ISABELLA: And what do you think about those anarchists who decided to form a group of women only called Mujeres Libres?

CONCHA: I didn't join that group. I was asked to, but I was very busy; I was a member of the Libertarian Youth, the trade union and the militia, I had no time.

ISABELLA: What kind of activities were carried out by the women of Mujeres Libres?

CONCHA: They focused on the freedom of women who, in some areas, were treated like slaves. They carried out important activities.

ISABELLA: They dealt with prostitution, abortion, education.

CONCHA: We all agreed upon these issues. I had always supported them.

ISABELLA: Concha, where did you go after the war?

CONCHA: It was tragic: we all moved to France; it took us several days to reach Port Bou.

ISABELLA: Where did you live?

CONCHA: I spent about nine months in a shelter in Northern France.

ISABELLA: Were you alone?

CONCHA: Yes, completely alone.

Then I went to the Argelès camp, where I stayed for over one year. I worked in an office and controlled the people coming in and out; I spent whole days writing names.

ISABELLA: Was this your job?

CONCHA: It was a voluntary work. Nobody forced us.

ISABELLA: How was life in the Argelès camp?

CONCHA: It was sad and hard, we could neither sleep well nor have a bath, since there was no water. Then things got better.

ISABELLA: Could you leave the camp?

CONCHA: We didn't know where to go. Our conditions were miserable; initially, we slept on the sand, then we built shacks with light, water and toilets.

ISABELLA: Were there anarchists, communists, and republicans?

CONCHA: Yes, you could meet anyone.

ISABELLA: Did the French government supply the meals?

CONCHA: Meals were mostly provided by the American Quakers.

ISABELLA: Did they visit the camp?

CONCHA: No, they sent them by post.

ISABELLA: Did they support you during your stay at the camp?

CONCHA: Yes, they strongly supported us. It wasn't easy to feed so many people. They sent food parcels and we distributed them; they also gave us a lot of clothing.

ISABELLA: After the year spent at the camp, what did you do? Did you return to Barcelona or remain in France? I know that in France you met the man with whom you had a baby.

CONCHA: Yes, but this happened at a later time. I was "claimed" by a French friend of mine with whom I used to hang out in Barcelona, so I was released. Then I moved from the camp to a place near Marseilles, a castle expropriated by the Mexican consulate for Spanish exiles.

ISABELLA: So you moved from the Argelès camp to a castle!

CONCHA: Yes, I stayed with my French friend for some time, then I went to one of the expropriated castles. One of them was inhabited only by women. One day, a voice on the speakers said that they were looking for nurses; I applied and there I met the man with whom I had a child; he was a doctor and worked there.

ISABELLA: Where did he come from?

CONCHA: From Madrid, but he lived in Barcelona.

ISABELLA: How did you meet?

CONCHA: I really liked the way in which he took care of the sick, and perhaps he felt the same thing for me.

ISABELLA: What was his name?

CONCHA: Isidoro Alonso. He was my second partner. I had left my previous partner, the member of the militia.

ISABELLA: I know that Isidoro went to Germany to fight against Hitler and you remained in France with the baby.

CONCHA: Yes, after Marseilles we moved to a small village in the Alps and there I realised that I was pregnant. We wanted to go back to Marseilles because I was not happy, it was very cold.

ISABELLA: When you returned to Marseilles, had you already given birth to your baby?

CONCHA: No, he was born there. I spent some months with the Quakers and then returned to Spain.

ISABELLA: What did you partner do?

CONCHA: He joined a clandestine group and tried to enter the area occupied by the Nazis. It was a hard mission; he left and I didn't know anything more about him. I assume that he died in Germany.

ISABELLA: Was he an anarchist too?

CONCHA: He was a socialist, he was somewhat oriented towards anarchism but he was more moderate. In any case, I think that we wouldn't have stayed together for a long time, there were too many differences between us.

ISABELLA: What's your son's name?

CONCHA: Ramón Alonso.

ISABELLA: So did you go back to Barcelona with your son?

CONCHA: Yes, but I don't remember the exact year.

ISABELLA: Did you stay in Spain even under Franco's regime?

CONCHA: Yes, when I came back, I was deprived of everything. They seized my mother's old house and we had to rent one: it was a tragedy.

ISABELLA: Why did you decide to return to Spain?

CONCHA: I had a small child and I was homesick. Some comrades of mine had returned and urged me to follow them.

ISABELLA: Had you got any family members in Barcelona?

CONCHA: There was my mother and two younger sisters.

ISABELLA: Was it hard?

CONCHA: With the benefit of hindsight, I wouldn't have returned; in France, things would have been better.

ISABELLA: There you experienced the terror of Francoism, didn't you?

CONCHA: Nothing happened to me, because they didn't denounce me, but the police came looking for my father and my brother. My father had escaped to France and never got permission to return and see his family. During the war, he was one of the members of the "control patrols", they were often executed.

ISABELLA: When you came here during the Franco regime, were you still involved in politics?

CONCHA: Of course, I've always devoted myself to politics. At that time, I had a market stall and sold costume jewellery at Sant Antoni fair; there I acted as a point of reference for many people: I collected packages, information and secrets. Fortunately, I wasn't denounced, although someone saw me attack the convent.

ISABELLA: What convent?

CONCHA: The Loreto convent, here in Barcelona, in the las Cortes district. We had sent the nuns away to turn the convent into a canteen.

ISABELLA: Did the nuns cooperate with you?

CONCHA: Only some of them, but generally they didn't act badly. I had to check the records, because some had stolen some money.

ISABELLA: And where did the nuns go?

CONCHA: They tried to settle down as best as they could; some stayed in Barcelona, while others went away, however, we hurt none of them.

ISABELLA: Did you personally take part in the attack on the convent?

CONCHA: Yes, of course! But we didn't mistreat anyone and there were no abuses.

ISABELLA: However, many churches were burnt down during the civil war.

CONCHA: Well, war is war. Even the convent was burnt down.

ISABELLA: After all, the Church didn't support the Republic.

CONCHA: No; the Church has always supported the fascists.

ISABELLA: As far as you know, were there any priests who denounced the anarchists?

CONCHA: No, but surely there were some.

ISABELLA: What did anarchism imply during the civil war? Did private property exist? Did anyone own anything?

CONCHA: The principles of anarchism were better applied in Aragon. There everything was collectivised: the lands, the factories, the working cycles. We all had enough food to survive and with the any surplus we bought cars and other items for the community. We also operated the factories, however, the owners benefited from it, because, after the war, they re-acquired their factories and made them work even better than before. This happened in the factory where I worked: the owner had two or three machines and, after the war, she had about ten, thanks to our work, there was a printing machine and one which produced lathes.

ISABELLA: So anarchism aimed at the collectivisation of the factories, the land and the whole economy; but, according to you, is this feasible?

CONCHA: We proved that it was feasible. In the factory where I worked, nobody was the boss, we collectively made our decisions during meetings.

ISABELLA: This article says that free love was more a theoretical issue than a practical one, what does it mean?

CONCHA: This is something I said during an interview which was published at a later time. The issue of free love was misunderstood; they thought that women could have sex with anyone, but it wasn't so!

ISABELLA: In these cases, there is always a double standard.

CONCHA: Men have always been free, however, there is a clear difference between freedom and being libertine; being free doesn't mean having sex with just anyone.

ISABELLA: Did the presence of a female minister, namely Federica Montseny, positively influence women's mind-set?

CONCHA: Yes, it paved the way for us.

ISABELLA: What was the opinion of male anarchists about the greater freedom of women? Did they support you?

CONCHA: Sometimes they supported us, but some still preferred having a slave at home. Nowadays, some are still very jealous and possessive, as if "their" women belonged to them. We are free, we don't belong to anyone.

ISABELLA: So you've always been a militant, both during the war and under Franco.

CONCHA: Yes, and still now. If there is a group, I'll join it. I still attend university when there is some debate; I don't go to parties at my time of life.

ISABELLA: How old are you, Concha?

CONCHA: Now I'm 95 years old.

ISABELLA: So your anarchist beliefs have not changed, have they?

CONCHA: Rather, it has strengthened.

ISABELLA: Anarchism spread here in Catalonia also because you put it into practice.

CONCHA: Yes, we established many libertarian universities here which acted as reference points for many women. Women didn't attend trade unions, unlike universities. On some occasions, there were even more women than men.

ISABELLA: Have you got any brothers or sisters?

CONCHA: I had an elder sister, but she was hit by meningitis and never recovered; I also had a brother who was four years older than me.

ISABELLA: And did your brother support your militancy?

CONCHA: Yes, of course! He was a militant in Sants, while I remained in Faros.

ISABELLA: You were talking about what your father did during the civil war.

CONCHA: Yes, he was a member of the control patrols.

ISABELLA: What happened to you during the events of May 1937? Were you here in Barcelona?

CONCHA: There were shootings everywhere, telephones didn't work and we didn't know what was happening. So a comrade of mine and I were sent to the Regional Committee in Via Layetana, but on the way, an Italian guy said, "I'll drive you there". His car looked like an army tank, but this was only its external appearance, because its interior had nothing to do with an army tank. As soon as we reached Via Layetana, they shot at us from all the corners. The Italian guy had a head injury and went to the hospital, I had several leg injuries; only some splinters could be pulled out.

ISABELLA: I didn't know that you were injured during the May events.

CONCHA: We had occupied the telephone exchange, but the Communists wanted to control it. There were so many deaths. The POUM militants were accused, since they had had some trouble with the communists, then Andreu Nin was tortured and killed. It was a tragedy.

ISABELLA: In your opinion, would you have won the war if this tragedy had not happened?

CONCHA: I don't know. I guess that we had already lost it. With the benefit of hindsight, things became clearer. Various countries had established agreements against the Republic, we couldn't win. We worked hard, but we didn't know what was happening around us. They would have won in any case. We couldn't win.

ISABELLA: Do you think that an anarchist society could be created today?

CONCHA: It would be hard but possible. Now people are more conformist, they don't fight for their ideas and actually have no ideas at all. Even those times were hard. At the factory where I worked, there was a small group who opposed the revolution. We had to fight against selfishness, against our own home, our own lives, our own spouse, our own families, and some didn't want to share what they had; and this still happens today. Anarchism is a great idea and I keep it in my heart, but theory and practice are not the same thing.

ISABELLA: I can feel that you're still very proud of your being an anarchist.

CONCHA: Yes, of course! We didn't achieve our goals, and I'm sorry for that, but at least we tried. I am very proud of what we tried to do. Most people didn't agree with our ideas, but we tried.

ISABELLA: If you could turn back time, would you change anything?

CONCHA: I would do exactly what I did; maybe something more.

ISABELLA: Are you still in contact with any woman from Mujeres Libres?

CONCHA: No, but I know that they are continuing their activity in France. Pepita Carpena, Blanca Navarro, Sara Guillén ... Sara's father was killed when she was very young and she wanted to join the militia, but she wasn't allowed to. Later she became a member of Mujeres Libres. She was the secretary of the group and did an excellent job.

ISABELLA: Yes, it was impressive: an organisation which involved 20,000 women.

CONCHA: I met many of them. Unfortunately, I was very busy and couldn't be with them. I was fighting on the front, and it was good for me.

ISABELLA: How did you psychologically react to the fact of killing a man, regardless of his being an enemy and a fascist?

CONCHA: Fortunately, I think that I never killed anyone, at least in cold blood. I often shot at the enemies ... but you didn't know the exact trajectories of the bullets. War is war; they shot at us and we did the same.

ISABELLA: It must have been hard for you, as a woman who lived in the Thirties, to shoulder a rifle and shoot.

CONCHA: Yes, it was hard. But I stood with my comrades.

ISABELLA: And after the father of your child, the man who died in Germany, had you had any other partner?

CONCHA: Yes! I have had a partner for the last 30 years.

ISABELLA: Do you believe in marriage?

CONCHA: No, getting married is pointless.

ISABELLA: What do you think about the fact that in Spain gay and lesbian people are claiming their right to marry?

CONCHA: I think that freedom should be granted to everyone.

ISABELLA: In other countries, they cannot marry, there are many prejudices.

CONCHA: And here, too! The Church always brings along prejudices. It opposes gay people; it regards it as a moral issue.

ISABELLA: Thank you Concha!

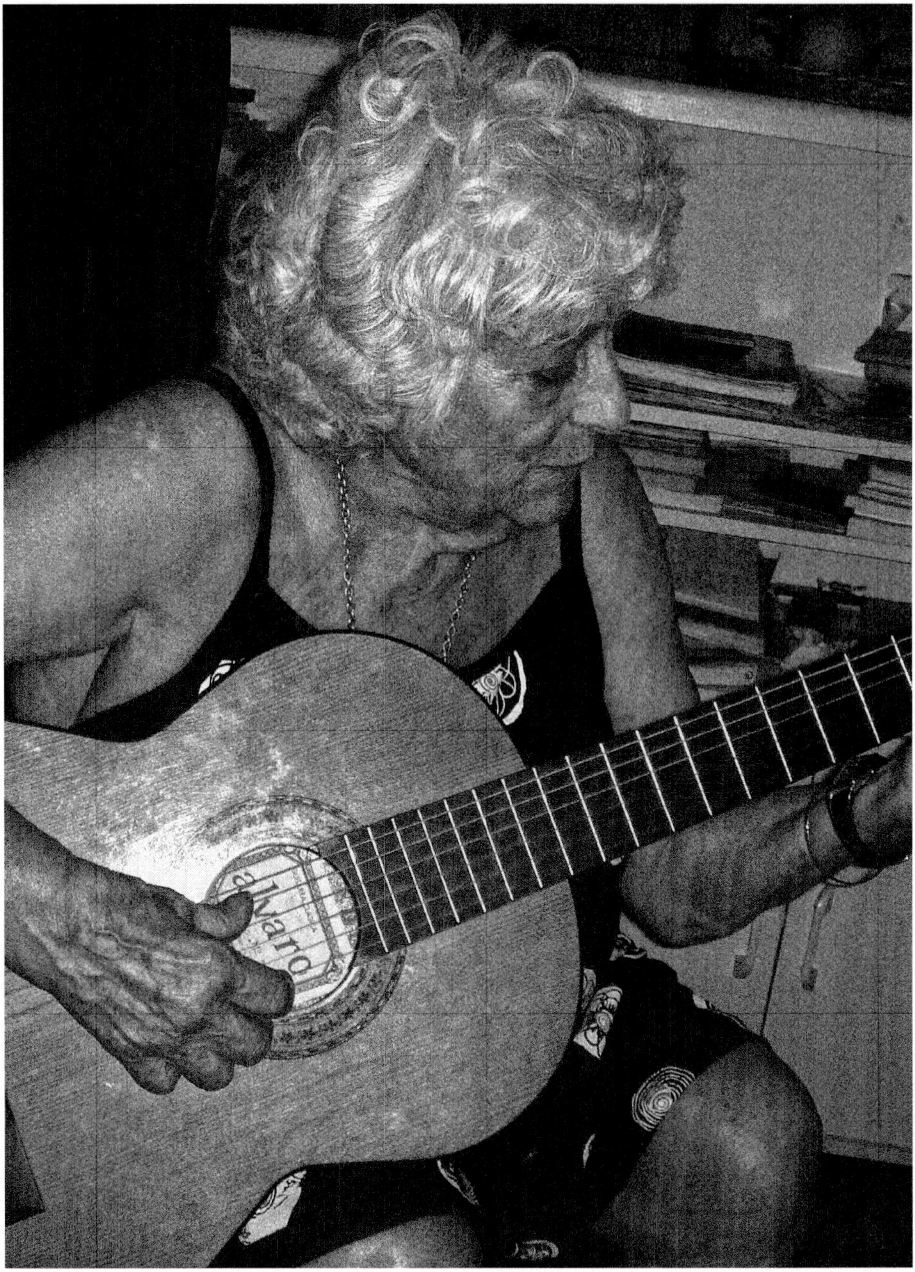
alvaro

TERESA REBULL

(1919-2015)
POUM | Interviewed June 2010, Banyuls-sur-Mer

Marta and I left Girona to go to Banyuls-sur-Mer, a picturesque town on the border between France and Catalonia. Teresa, a POUM militant and popular Catalan singer, welcomed us with her guitar and a tasty white coffee. "Allez-nous[1]" she said, and we were ready to start the interview.

ISABELLA: Hello Teresa, where and when were you born?

TERESA: I was born in Sabadell, near Barcelona, in 1919.

ISABELLA: Besides politics, I know that you are also interested in painting.

TERESA: I am interested in many things. Cezanne used to say that when you think that you have reached the highest painting skills, you actually have to start all over again.
　When I was just a young girl, but at that time, I had to work in the factory and couldn't spend time on my passions. Then, after the war and the exile, I attended a French school and started painting. Initially, I produced only a few paintings, but after May 1968, I said to myself, "The flower power time is over, now it's time for me to focus on protest painting, engagé art". I like painting, although paintings are purchased only by rich people, and if you want to make a living with art, you must agree to compromises.

ISABELLA: You have many passions — art, singing, painting.

TERESA: Yes, and I would also like to write books, but I'm not able; I could have learnt how to at school, but when I was 12 years old I was already working in a textile factory; I couldn't study.

ISABELLA: Did you stay in Sabadell?

---

1. Her version of the French phrase "Allons-y" — Let's get started

TERESA: No, during the Republic I moved to Barcelona because of work, and there I stayed at the Rebull house where I got in contact with the POUM.

ISABELLA: What do you mean?

TERESA: They were all members of the party. There was Manolo, Joaquín (Maurín)'s brother, whom I liked very much, although I eventually got married to José, his best friend. When we were sitting at the table, I played footsie with both José and with Manolo. It was all very silly.

ISABELLA: And what happened then?

TERESA: Manolo died because of the Stalinist repression. He was very ill, he was imprisoned and died at the Hospital of Saint Paul in Barcelona. Before he died, Pepe and I visited him and Manolo said, "Teresita, do you love José? Well, I do too". He died in Barcelona. Have you read the book that I wrote?

ISABELLA: No.

TERESA: I described what happened to Manolo. Once he was kept in a prison in Barcelona where there was a statue of Federico Soler Pitarra, a painter, in Carrer dels Escudellers.

ISABELLA: It must be Plaça George Orwell.

TERESA: The one who participated in the war? I'm not sure, maybe I'm referring to another place, I mean the Rambla with the Falcon hotel. This is where there was the prison where Manolo was kept and I used to stop in front of the statue and stare at him; he stood behind bars with a sad look. It was tragic and it was all because of the Stalinists — it was their fault we lost the revolution. Recently I've been interviewed by a Catalan broadcast channel and I've said that it was their fault!

ISABELLA: People need to hear your words, because it's not enough to read about these events in books; some important anecdotes may help us better understand how things really were.

TERESA: For example, I remember a German girl who supported the Russians.

ISABELLA: Was she a Stalinist?

TERESA: Yes, and she said that the Stalinists were right, she was manipulated by them. In Spain, people are mostly reformists and prefer being ruled by a right-wing party instead of a revolution. In the past, revolution was in the air, but now things are different. Do you know why? Because consumerism has switched our brain off.

ISABELLA: Let's go back to your personal events. So you arrived in Barcelona and met the Rebull family.

TERESA: Yes, Maurín and Rebull.

ISABELLA: Why was Maurín staying with the Rebull family?

TERESA: Because he was a friend of theirs. Pepe was a special man, a skilful planner, just like the whole Rebull family.

ISABELLA: You joined the BOC and then the POUM, is it right?

TERESA: No, when I became a member of it the POUM was already formed as a party.

ISABELLA: Did you also meet Maria Teresa Andrade?

TERESA: Yes, we were imprisoned in the same cell, together with Katia Landau and her partner, we were in Vía Layetana.

ISABELLA: When were you arrested?

TERESA: Before Andreu Nin was killed, after the events of May, when the repression against the POUM broke out.

ISABELLA: What were you doing at that time?

TERESA: I was working at the Generalitat and they watched over me every day. Teresa, Pilar Santiago, and all the POUM members were watched over. Pepe knew these things well and said, "When you leave your office, don't turn around; if someone is following you, change your itinerary". That's what I did, I got on and off the tram, they were cowards.

ISABELLA: And how did they arrest you?

TERESA: They arrested me at the POUM Socorro Rojo Committee. I had some documents for Solano. Pepe was ill and I replaced him. When I entered the committee, my comrades didn't greet me, then a Stalinist asked me, "What are you doing here?"

And I replied, "I must talk to the people who take care of the guys on the front". But I had been denounced, so they arrested and took me to the prison, where I met Maria Teresa.

ISABELLA: Where was this prison?

TERESA: It was in Vía Layetana, opposite the music palace, in front of the police station. In that prison, there were also some nuns and they were beaten too. But after eight days I was released, because my father asked about me — he was a member of the Communist party. When I was set free, he asked me to thank a soldier, but I refused.

ISABELLA: Was your father a member of the Communist party?

TERESA: Yes, he eventually became communist; we had many quarrels at home, but before he died, he said, "Forgive me for my mistakes". The Communist Party urged him to denounce me; initially, they were sympathetic, but then they even threatened him.

ISABELLA: That's awful!

TERESA: Did you know this?

ISABELLA: Yes, of course, but your words are impressive.

TERESA: Our personal experience cannot be manipulated.

ISABELLA: And now, how are you?

TERESA: From a psychological point of view, I'm fine, but my shoulder hurts, I suffer from arthritis, I'm not well.

ISABELLA: Let's go back to that time. You met José and married him.

TERESA: No, we didn't get married immediately; we got married in France, some years later, after the birth of our children. During the war, Pepe was a member of the militia and escaped to France with forged documents because he was persecuted.

ISABELLA: And how did he get forged documents?

TERESA: In this case, it was easy. He found some documents on the ground and just them picked them up with the aim of using them sooner or later. And he was right.

ISABELLA: Did he use them to cross the border?

TERESA: Yes, and to escape from the Stalinists. In France, he used the forged documents because we knew that the Stalinists would still persecute us. There he joined the resistance with a false name, became a member of the maquis and was caught by the Germans. They were looking for an Italian revolutionary and were about to arrest him, but Pepe managed to escape.

ISABELLA: Did this happen in France?

TERESA: Yes, in France, during the resistance against the Germans.

ISABELLA: When you crossed the Pyrenees, during the war, where did you settle down? In Banyuls-sur-Mer?

TERESA: No, we temporarily settled in Perpignan and then moved to Paris. We reached Perpignan on a truck with Andrade, Gironellas, and other comrades of the party, then we headed to Paris and everyone looked for a shelter.

ISABELLA: Gorkín went to Mexico.

TERESA: Yes, some of them went there — we had the chance to go to the United States, but we didn't want to leave our family.

ISABELLA: Did your parents stay in Barcelona?

TERESA: Yes, they were hidden and persecuted. We stayed in Paris and then moved to Marseilles and eventually joined the maquis guerrilla movement. During the liberation, I was in Paris and it was amazing. That time was hard, but also very exciting.

ISABELLA: When you crossed the French border, were your children already born?

TERESA: No, I was 19 years old, but ask me about political issues and let alone children, husbands, and boyfriends, otherwise we'll never finish!

ISABELLA: Your personal life is important too.

TERESA: Pepe and I hadn't got married yet when we left Spain; we got married many years later, when our children were already adults.

ISABELLA: We may focus on political issues, but, as a historian, I'm interested also in your personal events, how you experienced the war, how war changed your life. Had you ever met Nin in person?

TERESA: I met him before the POUM was established, because Nin used to come to Sabadell to hold lectures for the anarcho-syndicalists whom my parents had joined. When I met Nin, I was ten or eleven years old.

ISABELLA: Nin went to Russia and then returned to Spain, is that right?

TERESA: Yes, and he used to talk also about the situation in Russia, so information started to spread here too. Once I was invited to a concert in Germany and there I was given copies of the letters that Nin and Maurín wrote to each other. In 1921-1922, Nin was in Russia and told him that the situation was different from his expectations.

ISABELLA: This is also what comes out of the film "The Nikolai Case". It shows how Nin gradually changed his ideas about Russia and wanted to return to Spain after ten years in Moscow, but things were complicated.

TERESA: Nin was saddened and disappointed by what he had seen in Russia. In the Thirties, the POUM was already reporting on the crimes committed by Stalinism. Nin was such a kind man that I always get angry when I think about the fact that his corpse has never been found. During an interview, a journalist asked me, "What do you think about the war? Do you think that you would have won if socialists, communists and anarchists had joined forces?" I answered, "Let's set the record straight. It was neither the socialists' nor the anarchists' fault, the Communists ruined everything," and then I explained my opinion about the law of transition: who accepted the transition, who required it? It was Carrillo and everyone knows it.

Once I was in Paris and Elisa Serna[1] came singing with me; she was pleasant and very talented, but she was a Communist. Communists are like those Catholics who believe that the inquisition was terrible but necessary. We attended a large meeting at the university; there were many Communists there and she sang. I figured out that they wanted to make up with the Falange and the king; I didn't know what to think and she said, "We must turn the page," and I replied, "That's outrageous! Should we really forgive the Phalangists?"

ISABELLA: The Communist Party had a reformist attitude.

TERESA: Yes, one day I heard a debate about the recovery of historical memory, so I wrote to a newspaper and said that if they really wanted to recover some historical memory, then they might give us Nin's corpse back.

ISABELLA: That fact that his corpse has never been found is atrocious.

TERESA: Because nobody wants it to be found.

ISABELLA: Sometimes mass graves are discovered.

TERESA: Yes, this requires some investigation and nobody will ever carry them out, because they are afraid. My book was disruptive precisely because it deals with it and criticises Minister Vilella[2]. So it was withdrawn, because people are afraid when someone talks about the events which happened at that time.

ISABELLA: Maybe they just want to look forward.

TERESA: They are cowards. Moreover, Franco and Francoism have instilled the utmost obedience among the people. One of the Goytisolo[3] brothers once said, "It will take several generations to get rid of Francoism". Franco carried out the coup because he knew that we would have a revolution, there were uprisings in the streets due to the mess made by the Republic, owing to fear, indecision, a poor strategy, or because they were all middle-class people.

---

1. Serna was a well-known activist and protest singer towards the end of the Franco years.
2. Rafael Vidiella I Franch (1890-1982) was a Communist-aligned Catalonian minister during the war
3. Juan, Luis and Jose, prominent Spanish poets and writers.

ISABELLA: Many compromises were made with the Catholic Church and the landowners.

TERESA: Yes, they were undecided. And even before the Black Years, Maurín, who was a deputy then, warned us against what could have happened, especially about our imminent repression. There was an amazing revolutionary attitude and Franco was a soldier of the Republic; he was an official of the Republic and trained in Morocco.

ISABELLA: After all, the Moroccans repressed the revolt in Asturias.

TERESA: Yes, everything was organised there.

ISABELLA: Teresa, with whom were you in contact during the war? You have already mentioned Maria Teresa Andrade.

TERESA: Yes, the POUM had a women's secretariat and Maria Teresa Andrade managed the group. She was very kind and intelligent. She was a sort of legend. I'll tell you something about her. One day, when I was in prison, I went to the basement to go to the toilet, there was a narrow corridor, the wooden floor was full of pee and had a nauseating smell. Well, while I was walking, I suddenly heard, "Hey ... hey ... Teresitaaa ..." I thought that I was dreaming — perhaps the mice were moving and I heard my name. "Teresitaaaaa..." I was scared and ran away. Upstairs I met another woman and asked her, "Maybe I'm going crazy, but I heard someone calling my name". She went there but heard nothing, then I returned there and heard again, "Hey ... Teresita, I'm Maria Teresa". And she was there, poor woman, locked in a very narrow space where she couldn't even breathe and added, "We're all here!" Later they questioned us ...

ISABELLA: And were you tortured?

TERESA: Yes, obviously! After all, we had been arrested! Today I asked my sister to come and tell you about her husband who was killed by the Stalinists on the front, the so-called "el Campesino"[1] was there too.

---

1. Valentín González (1904-83) was a military commander heavily promoted by the Soviets but accused of brutality to his own side. After the war ended he fled to the USSR where he was accused of imcompetence and eventually sent to a gulag, escaping to Iran in 1949 and then France.

ISABELLA: Líster[1], the Stalinist.

TERESA: Yes, they showed my brother-in-law a document and wanted him to sign it, it said that Andreu Nin was a fascist. My brother-in-law replied, "I won't sign this document," and he was executed by firing squad.

ISABELLA: Was he your sister's husband?

TERESA: Yes, Pilar Santiago, too, could tell you many things.

ISABELLA: I met her several times and I've already interviewed her; they killed her husband based on the escape law.

TERESA: I was in Barcelona when this happened to her. Then, after we went into exile, we lost contact with one another.

ISABELLA: You mentioned the women's committee of the POUM.

TERESA: Yes, and it was very interesting.

ISABELLA: Who were the members of the group? Pilar Santiago ...

TERESA: Yes, there was Pilar, although I seldom saw her, because she was an intellectual. The group organised the workers, and Maria Teresa Andrade "trained" us, planned activities for the soldiers on the front and held art history and French lessons, it was amazing! I wrote an article published in a magazine and signed as Teresa Sorel; Rebull is my husband's surname. It was a feminist article; today I couldn't write it, but at that time I could. Pepe used to say that women should be independent, but as long as they stood with their husbands, they had to obey them. He was a dictator in his private life.

ISABELLA: Pepe Rebull?

TERESA: Yes, just like all the revolutionaries. My mother too was a very active woman who organised meetings and my father was an anarcho-syndicalist, but at home she had to obey him. He was a male chauvinist.

---

1. Enrique Líster was a Communist Party member and later commanded the 11th division of the Republican Army. He too fled to the USSR after the war, and served as a Red Army general in World War II.

I was talking about the repression in Barcelona in 1937; at that time there was the Negrín government and repression became even more heavy handed, they sent Largo Caballero away.

ISABELLA: He was sent away, because he didn't want to repress the POUM militants, he was an honest man, wasn't he?

TERESA: Many socialists were undecided, but Largo Caballero was respectable.

ISABELLA: Teresa, did you attend the trial?

TERESA: No, it was very dangerous. We had to be discreet. The police looked for me at my parents' house and asked my mother where I was. The repression was severe; moreover, we suffered hunger, because milk and food were distributed only to the officials. We ate stray cats so as not to starve. It was a horrible period and now they pay homage to Negrín. Why? What became of Spain's gold?

ISABELLA: It was sent to Russia.

TERESA: Yes, but apart from Russia it was distributed among the officials. Thanks to the Stalinists, we lost the chance to make the revolution, as shown by the Hitler-Stalin pact, but ask the experts for better explanations.

ISABELLA: Stalin didn't want to encourage a revolution.

TERESA: In Spain, the militia committees were already making revolution, there were many active groups, then the Russians imposed their "politics" and all our achievement were swept away. They gave uniforms to the soldiers but the soldiers in uniform didn't want a revolution, do you understand? Have you watched the Land and Liberty film? During the film there is a scene where a man leaves the POUM to join the Communists and his girlfriend learns about it.

ISABELLA: She finds his party card.

TERESA: It was very sad.

ISABELLA: Yes, but the POUM members, who have struggled against many things, are very close-knit.

TERESA: We respect and love one another; although we may lose contact with one another, because we keep in our heart this frustrated revolution for which we have struggled, all the difficulties that we have experienced, the amazing meetings, the affinity with our comrades, the family, and the institutions. This party really wanted to make the revolution, but also spread culture. Does this sound so strange?

ISABELLA: No, this is exciting.

MARTA: You are very clear headed!

ISABELLA: We've also met and interviewed Teresa Carbó.

TERESA: Is she still alive?

ISABELLA: Yes, she's 102 years old!

TERESA: Then I must absolutely visit her, I thought that she was dead. I'm so happy! I have not seen her for over ten years.

ISABELLA: We told her that we would come here today, and she asked us to greet you.

TERESA: Does she still live at the Laurels Rosas nursing home?

ISABELLA: Yes, and she's in good shape. I met her in 1995 and she told us many things about Nin.

TERESA: Teresa is a true revolutionary. We left Barcelona to drive to the border on an old truck, but the Stalinists wanted to take that too. I tried to get on, but they crushed my hands with their feet. Teresa saw them and started to shout wildly, we struggled to recover it and, eventually, we succeeded.

ISABELLA: This happened when you left Barcelona, didn't it?

TERESA: Yes, when Franco's troops had already arrived. It was terrible because women got into the truck and held their children on their laps. But then they had to get off because there wasn't enough room for everybody. It was atrocious. We seized that truck as if it were our life and

I had to reach Pepe who was waiting for me in Vic and I didn't want to get off. I couldn't even lay my feet out on the ground, since we were pressed against one another. Are you meeting anyone else besides me?

ISABELLA: We will meet Elvira Godás[1], whose brother was a POUM militant.

TERESA: Godás is amazing. I don't know if she remembers me, anyway, bring her a book from me.

ISABELLA: Of course!

TERESA: This book is written in Catalan.

ISABELLA: We'll also interview Pelai Pagés[2].

TERESA: Pelai is very intelligent, he knows everything. When I presented my book at the University of Barcelona, he supported me. Please, tell him that I was often on the point of calling him, but I couldn't do it. I didn't want to bother him. But I need him. From a political point of view I feel lonely here.

ISABELLA: I'll tell him as soon as I see him.

TERESA: Have you got any plans now?

ISABELLA: I would like to write an essay about the POUM women.

TERESA: The story of my life can be interesting. Our escape from the concentration camp was extraordinary. I'll tell you about it. My brother-in-law, David Rey, went to Mexico and stayed with Trotsky and Frida Kahlo. He knew that Trotsky was in danger.

ISABELLA: Everyone knew it, but nothing could be done, because Stalin's killers were always ready and alert.

TERESA: Trotsky didn't want to be watched over, he had an awkward character. Well, when we reached the French border, we saw the trucks

---
1. Godás played a major role in developing the Sceond Republic's educational programme.
2. Catalan historian and specialist in the history of POUM.

that carried people to the Argelès camps. At the time, we didn't know what kind of camps they were, but later we found out. Then Pepe said, "Let's stay here, on the top of the mountain". Suddenly, a policeman arrived and asked us for our documentation. Pepe answered, "We keep them in our suitcases, we'll go and get them!" The policeman followed us and Pepe said, "Let him go on". The policeman exclaimed, "Hurry up! Depechevous!" And Pepe replied: "Depeche-vous et allez-nous!" We started to run, jumped on a truck and escaped!

ISABELLA: You saved your lives!

TERESA: We seized this opportunity. Then we walked, hid ourselves, crossed mountains and hills, then entered a cottage and fell asleep. The locals supported us, it was wonderful.

ISABELLA: This anecdote is very important.

TERESA: We were amazed at the solidarity we encountered in that village. Then we left Perpignan and reached the house of Gironellas, where we met Andrade and the other POUM members. One day, at the market, I saw many policemen and, when we returned home, we discovered that they had all been arrested. I was desperate, then someone hugged me and said "don't cry, my dear, I'm here". It was Pepe, who had managed to escape from a moving truck.

ISABELLA: That's incredible.

TERESA: We looked for shelter and found a place infested by lice; we slept all pressed up against one another, there was a man affected by tuberculosis who spat blood. Pepe and I held each other and we ... we made love! It was beautiful. I remember it as if it were yesterday.

ISABELLA: That's nice!

TERESA: Yes, it was nice, it could be the plot of a film, couldn't it? A film about Stalinism, revolution, and the struggle of the people. A film full of music and emotion. I devoted myself to music; in France I even received a prize — I'm self-taught.

ISABELLA: You are a popular singer.

TERESA: I'm a revolutionary singer, they regard me as a militant singer who defends Catalonia and Spain; when I refer to my country, I call it the Iberian Peninsula. For me, language is like mother's milk, and if you love your country, you'll love all the other countries of the world. When I returned here, people avoided speaking Catalan because it was forbidden. I'm not afraid of anything, either of my comrades or of anyone. I did everything all by myself and I'm proud of it. Previously, I was a member of the Socialist Party, but now I've left it, because they are too bland — they keep their heads down instead of reacting to the insults of the right-wing parties. Today, everybody can establish a populist party under a semi-fascist regime.

ISABELLA: We are constantly threatened by unemployment, xenophobia, and fascism.

TERESA: This may be dangerous both in France and in Spain, but the French are more vigilant and combative.

ISABELLA: Yes, when they go on strike it is effective.

TERESA: Their rights are deeply rooted in the French Revolution. Mitterrand used to say, "The revolution is not over yet". Going back to my story, we escaped from the camp and arrived in Castelet full of lice. Then we got together and went to Paris where our comrades helped us a lot.

ISABELLA: And why did you come back here?

TERESA: In Paris, some friends of mine told me that here people danced the "sardana". I'm a "sardanist", I really like dancing to the extent that I had attended the Pauleta Pañez school in Barcelona when I was 16 years old. Pauleta was about eighty years old and taught us to dance. The sardana flows in my blood, like flamenco and painting.

ISABELLA: Your love for life comes from your soul. How did Pepe die?

TERESA: Pepe died in 1999 when he was 93. He wasn't ill and died in peace. He had some physical ailments and this caused problems for him, although eight days before he died he gave a lecture on capitalism. He had a clear opinion about the International Monetary Fund. He believed that cooperatives might be a solution. I'm angry because that intelligent man never wrote anything. I cannot forgive him. Trotsky always mentioned him. Pepe was a true revolutionary and there were many differences between them.

ISABELLA: Yes, even between Trotsky and Nin.

TERESA: When Franco's troops advanced, Pepe suggested to Durruti that they should join forces in Barcelona but neither the CNT nor the POUM agreed with him.

ISABELLA: Was Pepe a friend of Victor Alba?

TERESA: Yes, of course. Victor Alba was always at the Rebull's house. The teacher of Victor Alba was the greatest of the Rebull family; Victor loved my brother-in-law very much, he always visited him even before I went there.

ISABELLA: What activities were you and Pepe involved in?

TERESA: We did everything. Pepe worked as a porter at the port, then he worked as a guardian in a lady's house. Later the members of the resistance asked him to work as an accountant for the newspaper. He didn't want to accept, since that task seemed too demanding and he feared that the French would become jealous, but then he accepted. So he went to Paris and started working for the newspaper which was called "Le Franc Tireur" and I moved to a village near Marseilles. As soon as he found an apartment, I joined him. We lived in Paris for 35 years until we returned here in the '70s.

ISABELLA: You said that you experienced the May events in France.

TERESA: Yes, it was wonderful.

ISABELLA: What do you think about the Stalinists?

TERESA: I think that they should be honest and say, "We were wrong and now we want to correct our errors," but actually they aren't honest. We should gather together all the people who have socialist ideas, who demand change and oppose the "bureaucratism" trap but nobody knows how to do it because power corrupts, as has happened to those who have fought for the independence of Catalonia. It all went well until they reached about 25 per cent, then the bickering began. They exploited the people's ideas for their personal interests.

ISABELLA: Have you ever thought of returning to Barcelona or Sabadell?

TERESA: I have recently been to Barcelona for a special event dedicated to singers which was held at the music museum. I was invited and seized the opportunity to see some friends.

ISABELLA: Do you know any other POUM militants who live here?

TERESA: I think that they're almost all dead except for a few of the old members.

ISABELLA: I know that some POUM days will be organised in Barcelona in October.

TERESA: I didn't know that. Now, take what you want from this conversation, but please stress the fact that I'm not stuck in the past. I have evolved and have clear ideas on the current political situation. I would like all those who claim to be revolutionaries and socialists to speak out against capitalism and its lies. But nobody talks about this, nobody denounces the mafia inside the system.

ISABELLA: In Italy, there is a deep crisis which has involved even the press and journalists. But when I presented my book on the POUM, I noticed that many young people were interested in this topic.

TERESA: When you talk about the POUM, explain also what we wanted to do, don't just focus on the fact that we were victims of Stalinism. Don't forget to mention the situation in Spain at the time, our idea of revolution, our willingness to change the world, the lack of weapons and the imposed Stalinism.

ISABELLA: I remember the passion of Victor Alba when he told me that, in the past, workers could only lose their chains, while now they can also lose their car, mobile phone, and house.

TERESA: The revolution will come from Africa, where people suffer hunger and misery. Europe will be invaded by Africa and I hope I'll be there to welcome them with my arms wide open. We also fled to France and Mexico, but now we have all become middle-class people, including the workers and those who go to demonstrations. These demonstrations are fake, all activity in the country must be disrupted and no compromises must be accepted. And people know that. Are you in touch with Nin's daughter, who lives in Rome?

ISABELLA: No, but I'm in contact with her granddaughter, Silvia, who lives in London.

TERESA: I've known Nin's daughter since they were just children. Please, tell Silvia that I personally met her grandfather and now I miss him.

MARTA: You mentioned the female section of the POUM. Based on your experience, even in mixed groups, is there any difference between the militancy in women only groups and mixed groups?

TERESA: There was no difference. Moreover, my partner used to say that women cannot be independent if they are subjected to their husbands, if they don't work or are not the in control of their own lives. The POUM relied on this mind-set.

ISABELLA: Was he consistent with these ideas in his private life?

TERESA: From a political point of view, he was very coherent, unlike in his private life. When he discussed the liberation of women, I was 16-17 years old and he was 30. It was militant propaganda. He allowed me to do all that I wanted. Sometimes he wanted to be the boss but I started a little revolution at home. One day I wanted to sing. I took my guitar and said to him and my son, "I'm going to travel the world. Look after yourselves!" I said this when I realised that they didn't need me anymore and Pepe answered, "Where are you going? What are you doing?" He always set barriers to the impossible and I replied, "I don't know if I'll succeed, but I want to try," and I was very successful. I suffered from the lack of support from the people; I was discriminated against because I was a POUM militant, while the music industry is ruled by the members of the PSUC. One day, I was singing in Madrid, then some Communists entered the hall and shouted, "This woman cannot sing!" I was boycotted. I've never seen them here again, but they hate us. However, remember that the revolution will begin in Africa. When I was interviewed on a television broadcast, I said that everyone should run out on the streets and cry, "Revolution!" but this part of the interview was censored.

MARTA: Teresa, I'm interested in your story: a POUM militant who becomes an artist.

TERESA: I didn't ask any permission to do what I did.

MARTA: Who were your sources of inspiration?

TERESA: Nobody, I did it all by myself. I was proud to defend Catalan culture ruined by Franco and, through my protest songs, I claimed these things. I sang in Catalan and called for freedom. I was arrested twice due to my songs. I was charged with subversive pornography because I used to sing some poems by Raimón entitled "Cançons d'amor" dealing with eroticism. They were amazingly beautiful. The police arrested me in Asturias and asked me about the words, "What does the poet say? What does this mean?" I answered, "He is a poet who talks about love". They exclaimed, "Here in Spain we know what love is". "Yes, you know it. But you cannot express it as he does".

The police commissioner remained silent. He didn't know what to ask and I thought that I had to keep on fighting, since there was still much to be done. I did everything all by myself, nobody helped me.

MARTA: There's a clear difference between the people who remained in Catalonia and those who went into exile; your energy and utopianism are still alive.

TERESA: In Spain, we enjoyed a certain degree of freedom, while in France society was more "civilised". You should discuss this issue with my sister who stayed in Catalonia. She is 85 years old and she is still influenced by the Francoist repression; she is also repressed from a sexual point of view and realised what Franco did to her youth. In my songs I say, "Make love, love each other!" because making love makes you feel alive and strong. My sister is aware of the fact that she and many other women weren't free because of Francoism.

MARTA: Some years ago, Isabella and I met Pepita Carpena in Marseilles and your strength reminds us of her. She was an anarchist and member of Mujeres Libres. Were you in contact with anarchist women?

TERESA: Not much, unlike my parents, who were anarcho-syndicalists. The POUM was in touch with the CNT committee. We staged theatre shows together and carried out cultural initiatives, even when we lived in Paris. The anarchists who moved here are very conformist; probably you won't be surprised by my words, but many people were anarchists and now are boring middle-class individuals. Sometimes I talk to the anarchist refugees, but they don't understand me and say, "Stop talking like that, times have changed".

MARTA: The surprising thing is that you have updated your ideas and kept up with the times. Some are still living in 1936 but you are here in the now. Do you think that this is connected to the fact that you're an artist?

TERESA: Or maybe to my perseverance. In my songs, I express my ideas without any compromise. I touch the soul of the people without issuing any propaganda. Because the words written on the flyers soon get forgotten, while my songs will last forever. My activity was recognised some years later, in 2006, in Palau della Musica catalan, when a special event was organised to celebrate me. It was amazing, all my colleagues were there: Raimona Blue, Luís Llar, Maria del Mar Bune. Many singers participated and sang my songs.

MARTA: You have clear ideas about politics as they are today. You are not stuck in the past but you started a process to bring your thinking up-to-date. You defended your work as a woman and as an artist. Are these two natures somehow intertwined? I mean, has this to do with your spirit of rebellion?

TERSA: These things go hand in hand, they cannot be separated. However, there was no presumption. I've always done what I wanted. I sang what I wanted, I said what I thought. I've always expressed my ideas with the utmost freedom. I've never accepted any compromise. In Paris, I was told once, "If you sing in French, we'll organise some concerts". But I said no, because this is dangerous. This reminds me of a Portuguese girl who came here to sing. She had a lot of success and got a big head, but she lost everything in a few days, because she acted as a diva, as a duchess. I don't like this ephemeral world. I've never wanted to be an artist. I am a militant first and foremost. I sang, danced and painted, but I always remained a militant.

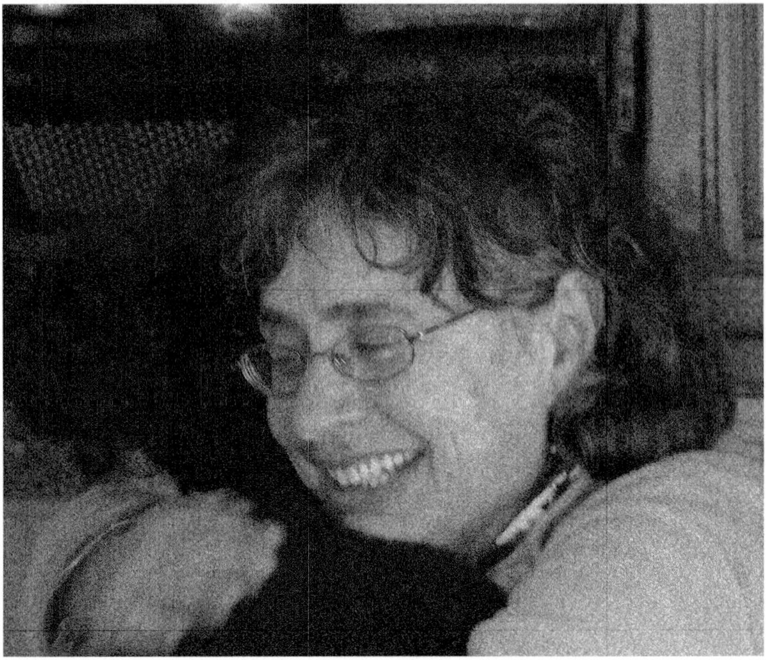

CRISTINA SIMÓN NIN

Catalan feminist
Interviewed December 2010, Esterri d'Àneu

Marta Alier and I travelled to the Pyrenees to interview Cristina Simón Nin, the granddaughter of Andreu Nin, the leader of the POUM, tragically kidnapped and tortured by Stalinist murderers during the civil war. She helped us discover the mysteries of Nin, of the young revolutionary who said to his partner, "I'm going to Moscow for a while, but I'll be right back," and returned home ten years later with another woman and their children.

CRISTINA: It's the first time I've stood in front of the camera.

ISABELLA: There a first time for everything, what's your full name?

CRISTINA: Cristina Simón Spinoza.

ISABELLA: Did you ever meet your grandfather?

CRISTINA: No, unfortunately Nin was killed in 1937 and I was born in 1959; that's why I don't know many things.

ISABELLA: Evidently, you don't have any personal memories but did your father ever tell you anything about him?

CRISTINA: He told us that, after Franco's death, he would explain many things because we should not reveal our family relationship with Nin. It was too dangerous.

ISABELLA: So didn't he tell you where your grandfather was?

CRISTINA: No, because I was very young, but my mother knew and when my father died, she told us everything. I was about 13 years old, my brother fourteen, and she suggested we should talk to my aunt who was Andreu Nin's eldest daughter. When we went to her there was a tense atmosphere because her husband was a Phalangist.

When we had finished our dinner I abruptly asked her, "Aunt, can you tell us something about our grandfather, about Andreu Nin?" She stiffened and answered, "I don't know who you're talking about. Your grandfather was a wine merchant from Reus. His name was Israel Simón". I insisted, "Our mother told us ..." and she interrupted me, "Your mother may tell you whatever she wants; now leave me alone!" We never returned to the subject and I did my studies with books and magazines but there was nothing about the POUM or Nin. So I asked for help at my school.

ISABELLA: Where did you live?

CRISTINA: When I attended secondary school I studied in Barcelona. We had a scholarship at a French school because my father didn't want us to go to a Francoist school and live in a self-righteous environment. The French school in Barcelona brought together many people who opposed the regime: there were the children of Republicans, of Communists, of the POUM militants, of anarchists. It was our shelter. Many people carried out research on their family history. I remember a boy called Albert Solé who helped us trace the history of our families, but we often failed. There was also another girl whose parents were PSUC members and we daydreamed about the past, figuring out situations that didn't correspond to reality. It was the need to create our own identity. So the years passed by and Franco died. I devoted myself to politics, but then I decided to move to the mountains and set it all aside.

ISABELLA: Could you get back to the personal story of your grandfather and his first partner?

CRISTINA: No, because my grandmother ...

ISABELLA: What was her name?

CRISTINA: Maria Andreu Baiget, she came from Vendreill (Tarragona) like him.

ISABELLA: Did they come from the same village?

CRISTINA: They met at school. They were both teachers but she was a little older than him. I've found it hard to reconstruct the whole story. I don't know much about my grandmother.

She was an anarchist, a very courageous woman with strong ideas, and I think that their families both opposed their relationship, precisely because she was older than him.

ISABELLA: Was she much older than him?

CRISTINA: She was about seven or eight years older than him. But this was a scandal at that time. They didn't get married and moved to Barcelona. My grandmother got pregnant and Andreu Nin went to Egypt to work. Did you know this?

ISABELLA: No, I didn't.

CRISTINA: Andreu Nin lived in Cairo for one year and worked for a textile company. I still keep the telegram that Nin sent to my grandmother from Cairo for my aunt's first birthday. Nin tried to keep in touch with his family, but there were some problems within the company and he returned home. As far as I know, Andreu Nin and my grandmother often quarrelled but they really loved each other.

They stayed together for ten or 12 years. When my father was born, Andreu Nin was already a militant and risked being imprisoned. When my grandmother was pregnant, she often visited him in prison. She used to hide small paper notes in her hair and gave them to him. She was very courageous.

ISABELLA: Did she get married again after the end of her relationship with Nin?

CRISTINA: Yes; with Ismael Simón, a wine merchant from Reus. I was told that he was a good father and gave his name to Andreu Nin's children — the children of a persecuted revolutionary who lived under the Francoist regime. The only thing that I know about this man is that he was an anarchist and a vegetarian. He was the second partner of my grandmother because Andreu Nin told her that he was going to Moscow for a couple of months but actually stayed there for ten years. Then he came back with another woman and other children and my grandmother told him to get lost.

ISABELLA: Do you know if Nin tried to get in touch with your grandmother during his stay in Moscow?

CRISTINA: It was hard to reconstruct the events of that period. Before my aunt died, I saw her once and said, "Today I would like to talk" and then I also talked to another aunt and with Wile, so I was eventually able to reconstruct what happened. When Andreu Nin arrived in Barcelona, after a ten year stay in Russia, he got in touch with my grandmother although he was with Olga, his new partner. Evidently, he didn't want to resume his relationship with my grandmother but he wanted to see and take care of his children. She was very angry but Nin managed to see my father. Later my father told his wife, my mother, that Nin wasn't a great father but was surely a great man. He recognised Ismael Simón as his father, because he bought him shoes in winter and helped him with his homework, but he was fascinated by Nin. Everyone also knew who my grandfather was because my father was an aviator during the Republic.

ISABELLA: He was very young.

CRISTINA: Yes, he began to fly with Joseph Canuda and Pepa Colomer[1]; at that time, the aviators attended training courses in Moscow and my father was asked, "Aren't you going on the course?" and he replied, "I cannot, because I'm Andreu Nin's son and I wouldn't come back home safe and sound from Moscow".

When I saw the "The Nikolai case" film I searched for the Russian daughters of Nin — Nora and Ida. I got in touch with Montserrat, the film director and she gave me Nora's telephone number and address. My head was in a whirl because I was thinking, "What am I doing? Should I call her?" Let's imagine that someone calls you and says, "Good morning, I am the Catalan branch of the Nin family". So I decided to write her a letter. After some time I still had not received a reply so I thought that Nora didn't want to meet me. But she had gone to London to visit her daughter Silvia and she called me immediately as soon as she returned home. I was at home and the phone rang. I answered and she said, "Hello, it's Nora Nin!" I was so excited!

We talked for a long time and then we kept in touch. Finally I had discovered a part of my personal story. Nora also called Ida, her other sister who lives in the United States and when I met Silvia in London, I was thrilled. Nora said, "You really must meet Silvia because you are so alike not only from a physical point of view. You'll get along well". Silvia also studied at the French secondary school — evidently some

---

1. Maria Josep Colomer i Luque was the first female flight instructor in Spain

things are inevitably handed down within a family in some way. We shared many things, such as 50% of the same books, while the others were complementary. Obviously, her books were in English and Italian, while mine were in French, Catalan and Castilian. It was really exciting to meet and exchange information, holding a box full of photos!

ISABELLA: When did you learn or realise that your grandfather was Andreu Nin?

CRISTINA: I discovered it gradually over the years. I started doing research in books. I knew of the Nin Foundation but it wasn't easy to find it and initially I was excited by any information about Nin. Moreover, my relatives used to tell me that I was a revolutionary like my grandfather! And I thought that this man couldn't have been a hero, because he wasn't a good father, and I didn't want to put him on a pedestal. I wanted to know how he really was as a man, so I trod carefully. But I found out impressive things about him. And the story deeply involved me because any criticism of him came from the Stalinists or the fascists and was groundless. Then a friend of mine watched the "Land and Freedom" film and said, "You absolutely must see this film!" Finally, I watched it and, although it doesn't deal with my grandfather, I was deeply impressed by the plot. I started to put together some things from George Orwell's *1984* and *Homage to Catalonia*, of which I had a complete edition that was forbidden here, as well as from *Land and Freedom*. Eventually, I watched *The Nikolai Case* and I found it amazing!

ISABELLA: It must have been very challenging and time-consuming research.

CRISTINA: Yes, going to Moscow, skimming all the archives and searching for information. Genovés told me that it was one of the most interesting things he did in his whole life.

ISABELLA: Is she a Catalan journalist?

CRISTINA: Yes, she's Catalan.

ISABELLA: Why did she shoot such a documentary?

CRISTINA: I didn't ask her as I never met her. We only spoke on the phone but she gave me the address of Nora Nin.

ISABELLA: Who financed this documentary?

CRISTINA: The TV3 Catalan Television. Ricard Bellis and Dolors Genovés went to Moscow to carry out this research and read hundreds and thousands of documents. They were about to give up but suddenly found the whole Nikolai file on the case of Andreu Nin. This is surprising, isn't it? This happened also to those who told the story of the POUM.

ISABELLA: When everything seems to be lost something special happens.

CRISTINA: The resilience of these people is impressive. They weren't eliminated in 1937 and weren't involved in the mechanisms of power, therefore they were not spoilt and never acquired the middle-class way of thinking. Then after my grandfather was tortured and killed, they felt even more obliged to remain loyal to the ideas of the group. These revolutionaries have never given up. And the POUM members endured the unbearable.

You have met them, you know how they are: they have a direct approach and a welcoming attitude towards people in spite of what happened to them. They were accused of being fascist traitors but withstood any attack. I really appreciate them.

ISABELLA: What is the most exciting thing about your grandfather's life?

CRISTINA: There are so many exciting things, for example, when he decided to enter the government or when he became Councillor of Justice. I cannot regard him as someone living with a gun in his pocket and risking his life. However, he even faced up to Stalin — fully aware of the consequences. They said, "Be careful or they'll kill you," he answered, "They won't be able to". But they arrested and tortured him. Wilebaldo (Solano) always cries whenever he tells this story. I cannot even imagine what they had to endure — torture, pain, violence. When I think about this, I cannot even sleep. I often think of him as well as of the death of his daughters in Moscow. Then I think of Nora, of the few memories that she has of her father, of the letters that he wrote to his mother where he tells her about his life in Moscow with Olga and their little children. These letters reveal Nin's "domestic" side, a man who loved his family and suffered for the daughters he could not have. I often think about their hardships; the problems with Trotsky due to the political differences arising from so-called "entryism"; although they were hard political enemies, my grandfather sought political asylum for him in Catalonia. I mean, in spite of their different political ideas, Nin was ready to help him. I feel small compared to him and it's hard for me to live up to this high family level. Moreover, even my father was highly esteemed.

ISABELLA: He was said to be a well thought out man.

CRISTINA: He was very kind and idealistic. Sometimes I think that he was idealized when he died, so I don't want to turn him into a hero who actually doesn't exist, but I still have beautiful memories of him.

ISABELLA: Have you got any other sisters?

CRISTINA: I have got a half-sister — we have the same mother. She is interested in the history of the POUM as well. Some days ago I took a picture of my son during an exhibition about the POUM and then I compared the three faces: his, Wilebaldo's and Nin's. Even my son rejected the POUM and Nin for some time, after all, he already had to face his adolescence problems, but now he is becoming increasingly interested in these issues.

ISABELLA: You discovered the truth gradually.

CRISTINA: Yes, over the years. I experienced Franco's dictatorship, unlike my son Isaac. However, I've also noticed "family" things that nobody tells you but cannot be denied. I had to reconstruct my story because I felt as if some pieces were missing. When my father died I was very young. So it was hard for me to trace my grandfather's story. As soon as I started collecting information I realised that the civil war and the post-war period were really hard. Moreover, I wanted to know where I come from and unveil the mysteries of my family.

ISABELLA: How did your life change after you discovered that you had such a heroic grandfather?

CRISTINA: I was asked the same question by the members of the Nin Foundation. They asked me, "How does it feel to have such a popular grandfather?" Well, I have no merit, since he was the hero; but having such a renowned grandfather is a great responsibility which urges you to be more honest and upright. I am Andreu Nin's granddaughter but I refuse any privilege. Having a famous grandfather, mother or father is nothing special in itself. However, I felt a need to reconstruct my story. And I also wanted to meet Carrillo and give him a piece of my mind.

ISABELLA: Carrillo?

CRISTINA: Yes, I would like to ask him his opinion of that time and now. I was told that if Carrillo meets me, he will probably recite a monologue and will avoid any personal contact. I would like to know how it feels to decide the fate of people. Perhaps he didn't realise what he was doing. But, although his Stalinist beliefs convinced him of the necessity to kill some people for the interests of the party, why has he never recognised the damage that he caused and never suggested any remedy over time? Wilebaldo told me that he privately apologised to him but I have never heard any public mea culpa.

ISABELLA: Did Wilebaldo meet him?

CRISTINA: Yes, probably in the '80s, but Maria Teresa surely has more information about this.

ISABELLA: But he should apologise publicly, shouldn't he?

CRISTINA: After so many years, it's the least that he should do.

ISABELLA: Personal apologies are useless because he made political mistakes.

CRISTINA: I've never heard any public apology from the PSUC members. They just keep on avoiding any debate. One day, I was introduced to Juan Saura from Initiative and he said, "So you are Andreu Nin's granddaughter, aren't you?" And he said nothing more, so I felt indignant. It is painful to realise that, after all the suffering that they caused, they cannot even say, "We were wrong". This is painful not only from the ideological and political perspective but especially from a personal point of view, because many families were destroyed by so much hatred and we cannot act as if nothing had happened.

ISABELLA: A political speculation and a rhetorical question: do you think that the war could have been won if there had not been such repression?

CRISTINA: I have often thought about it and I also asked for my son's opinion, because he asked me what would have happened if Franco had not won and if Stalin had not opposed the POUM and the anarchist movement and if they had join forces against the fascists. Then, after a lot of thought, I came to the conclusion that if the Republic had not lost the war, if Stalin had not intervened, and if the anarchists had continued the collectivisation with the POUM militants, and so on, the revolutionary state wouldn't have survived in any case. The capitalist countries would have destroyed it somehow. Without Stalin, the United States or the Allies would have intervened and the Republic would have been destroyed through politics, with weapons and by means of economic measures, because revolutionary states cannot exist.

The capitalist system cannot tolerate the success of another system. In *Homage to Catalonia* Orwell described an important thing that impressed me a lot: when he joined the POUM militia, he believed that his comrades were crazy, because they discussed everything and slowed down the decision-making process. "You're getting nowhere", he thought. But, eventually, he believed that this was the only way to fight against the fascists. Sometimes it is necessary to defer a decision, whilst in other cases, when there is unanimity, you must go on, being aware that there are no better alternatives. However, capitalism cannot accept any other system. Without the Stalinists or the fascists others might have intervened. Revolutionary states like this are too dangerous and the world economy cannot accept them and that's what is happening now to those who occupy houses and buildings.

ISABELLA: What is the most fascinating fact about the POUM? Collectivisations, the struggles of women, the militia?

CRISTINA: Militias were good, because they were an attempt to establish a horizontal structure even on the battlefield. Teresa Rebull told us that the women asked Mika Etchébère to stay with her because the Communists just made them wash the soldiers' clothes. Moreover, the POUM members were interested in culture and education. Among them there were many teachers and lovers of culture. And then there was machismo, which was deeply rooted in people, even in the revolutionary contexts. But the POUM women were very courageous and never accepted any compromises. They were forward-looking and this impresses me a lot. Eventually, it is worth mentioning the decision made by my grandfather when he was the Councillor of Justice: he changed the age of majority to 18 and supported the abortion law.

ISABELLA: What was the age of majority before that decision?

CRISTINA: 24 for women and 21 for men. He changed it to 18 for everybody; he was the first councillor who did this; moreover he supported the divorce and abortion law ...

ISABELLA: In your opinion, what was the difference between the POUM members and the anarchists?

CRISTINA: I think that there were few differences between them, since the two groups were very similar to each other in terms of organisation and revolution. Perhaps the POUM militants were less prone to armed intervention than the anarchists. But this is only partially true. The anarchists were regarded as people only able to throw bombs but it wasn't so. I cannot see any difference between the two groups. Perhaps, from an ideological point of view, it was easier for the POUM members to enter the government, while for the anarchists this decision was extremely painful. Most of the POUM members came from the trade union and were accustomed to struggles. It's hard to find differences between the two groups.

ISABELLA: Have you analysed the way in which the POUM members treated women? Was there a true equality between them?

CRISTINA: Yes, but only at a theoretical level. We attended a debate on the POUM women and realised that things were harder than we expected. That's why I would like to know my grandfather's attitude towards this issue, because my grandmother first and then Olga took care of the children. He was never at home. And they were militants too. It's always hard to change and give up a certain mind-set. Perhaps men really wanted to be less male chauvinists, but the education that they had received couldn't be swept away, so they also had to fight against themselves; but women were aware of this and didn't want to bow down. They refused to say, "We'll wash your clothes because we're women, that's what we do". They fought against the mistakes made until then. As evidenced by your interviews, when you meet a man and a woman from the POUM, the man is surprised because you pay the same attention to both of them, without any special treatment granted to him. Men get angry when they are treated in the same way as women, and it's up to you to highlight this difference. Even among the anarchists, there were these differences. I remember an anarchist woman from Mujeres Libres who said that special attention should be paid to sex, because this leads to machismo. In the end, many women kept away from the fighting and didn't leave for the front.

ISABELLA: Do you know anything about women like Mika Etchébère, who left for the front?

CRISTINA: I know very little about her. I just learnt some things from books.

ISABELLA: What do you think about her?

CRISTINA: Actually she was there with her partner and took charge of the militia when he died.

ISABELLA: Ippolitio Etchébère.

CRISTINA: I was surprised by her decision to take on the surname of her partner. This shows that there wasn't perfect equality.

ISABELLA: They got married ...

CRISTINA: Yes, but should women lose their surname after getting married? We always use male surnames, and this is not right. She could have changed things, but did nothing, that's what I think. After all, she was Jewish and Jews were persecuted, she must have suffered a lot. I don't know what I would have done if I had lived in 1936, because for me female soldiers make no sense: they cannot kill the children of other women! If I had been born at that time, I would have escaped the war, or maybe not, I don't know. But I cannot understand why women should join the army and take part in "peace missions" in Afghanistan, are they crazy? The same applies to policewomen. I don't understand.

ISABELLA: But leading a revolutionary militia is different, it broke the mould!

CRISTINA: Yes, it actually did at that time.

ISABELLA: Mika wrote a book about her story.

CRISTINA: I've never read it but I would like to know some more about her. It's worth finding out about what she did and letting people know. Little is known about the POUM women but research always helps to reveal more information.

ISABELLA: Among all the women I have met and interviewed, there is one who was the last person to see your grandfather Andreu Nin.

CRISTINA: Yes, she died recently.

ISABELLA: Teresa Carbódie? I interviewed her a short time ago.

CRISTINA: Yes, at the end of October.

ISABELLA: I didn't know, I'm sorry. With regard to courage, you must have appreciated the courage of your grandfather who didn't denounce anyone in spite of torture. This is an important legacy for the history of the POUM and all the militants. In your opinion, what made your grandfather act like that? If he had signed under torture, everyone would have understood the reason for his decision but he didn't sign.

CRISTINA: You must be very self-confident to behave like that. You must also love yourself and others very much to withstand torture. Somehow you give yourself permission to endure it.

ISABELLA: You will die anyway, but, under torture, you would do anything to get some respite. But Nin didn't give up.

CRISTINA: If you really believe in yourself and in others then you can even withstand torture. I don't know what it feels like. I can't even imagine because I've never experienced such a situation and I hope I'll never have to. I don't know how he could remain loyal to his love for life, to justice, to freedom, and also to his comrades. And they tortured him to the extent that he died ...

ISABELLA: And his body was never found ...

CRISTINA: There are many versions; some say that he was thrown into the sea.

ISABELLA: It's unlikely, Alcalá is far from the sea.

CRISTINA: Yes, but they say that Nin's corpse was brought to Valencia, where it was loaded aboard a ship and then thrown in the sea. But I must read this version again, because I cannot believe it. I don't know the truth:

it reminds me of the story of Anastasia, the daughter of the Russian tsar: nobody knew where she was and the legend says that she was finally found with her brother. Sometimes I think that it doesn't matter where Nin's corpse is, because I don't need to bring flowers to his tomb in a cemetery. But I cannot bear the idea of him having been buried in a mass grave. I would like him to have a place to rest in peace.

ISABELLA: If you could talk to your grandfather now, what would you tell him?

CRISTINA: Well, I don't know! I would say, "Sit down here and let's talk!" First of all, I would ask him many things about his personal life, what he thought at the time, how his ideas changed. Then I would ask him something about his relationship with my grandmother and his children, whether he liked to sing in the shower, and things like that. Eventually, I would like to learn more about his passion for foreign languages.

ISABELLA: He translated many books, didn't he?

CRISTINA: He was a very skilful translator; he translated Tolstoy, Dostoevsky, Chekov, and many other authors. Moreover, he could proficiently write and speak Russian, Catalan, and Castilian. I would have liked to ask him something about this side of him, because a passion for foreign languages is a peculiar characteristic of our family. Then I would ask him what happened to him in Moscow, how he met Olga, who Olga was, what the Russian winter was like and simple things like that. How he could endure torture, what he was like as a man. I would simply like to know some more about him. But my grandmother shouldn't be forgotten as well; she must have had a very strong character. She established a school all by herself and made a living from her work. She must have been very resourceful.

ISABELLA: Was she a teacher?

CRISTINA: Yes, and she established a school.

ISABELLA: I'm sure that nobody supported her.

CRISTINA: Yes, she suffered so much after he left and didn't come back. He left her alone with two children and went to Russia. Then she got married to Ismael Simón. But I would like to know how she felt when my grandfather finally came back after ten years. If I had lived with my grandparents, I would have learnt all these things, but I also lost my father. I can imagine many things or maybe I invent them. My grandfather was undoubtedly a great hero, but my grandmother shouldn't be forgotten. If you type Andreu Nin on a web search engine you'll find 3,000 pages, but nothing is said about María Andreu Baiget.

ISABELLA: Have you got some photos of when they were together?

CRISTINA: No, I only have a picture of Andreu Nin's mother, my great-grandmother, with a dedication to her grandchildren, namely to Maria Antonia and Carlos, who are my aunt and my father. It's the only document on which I can rely, because they tore up many photos. Moreover, I have some pictures of my father and my aunt, but I have no photos of Andreu Nin with his children. I sometimes wonder what they looked like. I would like to ask my grandmother, my grandfather, and my father many things. When my father died, I had not been able to ask him anything, because I was a child.

ISABELLA: How did he die?

CRISTINA: He died in an aviation accident. My father was an aviator, once, his plane hit a wire and he died. I couldn't ask him anything, I could only see his books. I know that he was an interesting, sensitive and intelligent man.

María Manonelles
(1913-2004)
POUM | Interviewed in June 1996

Manonelles was born in Mollerussa (Lleida) in 1913 and died in France, in Conflent-Conflans in 2004. She first joined the Catalan BOC of Maurín and thought that it would never have to merge with the Communists. She left it in 1935 to found the POUM (a party with which she never fully identified, because of the presence of Trotskyists, or former Trotskyists) — she would have preferred to be a militant in a more openly Catalan group.

During the civil war she was with the militia, on the Aragon front, and participated, directly or indirectly, in different military actions. After July 1937, with the Stalinist repression and the dissolution of the militia, she followed the political vicissitudes of her husband Josep Rovira, being arrested several times the Stalinist police, accused of being a "fascist and traitor".

After the end of the civil war she lived in France for a few months with her husband, but returned to Spain, during the Franco regime, to take care of her parents and raise her children. In Barcelona she participated in clandestine anti-Franco groups. After the end of the dictatorship, she returned to legally engage in politics.

She held several conversations with Ken Loach for the production of *Land and Freedom*, to discuss the conditions of life at the front, personal and political relations in the militias and the role of women within organisations of Spanish revolutionaries during the civil war.

MARÍA: What kind of research work are you doing?

ISABELLA: I am analysing the history of the POUM from 1935, the year it was founded, until 1937, when it was declared illegal.

MARÍA: I have to tell you that the history of our party is much longer and more complex than what those two years of history can represent. The POUM was not born in September 1935, nor did its history end in June 1937. Before the merge with the communist left, most of us were active in the BOC, the Workers and Peasants Bloc, which had a Catalan approach. After June 1937 all the POUM militants who escaped the Stalinist repression continued to militate, although illegally, until the end of the civil war and even later, during the Franco regime. The history of our party cannot be understood and analysed if the period of secrecy that lasted about 40 years is not considered. If the history of the party is analysed during the "legality", you run the risk of analysing a rather limited period that lasted a little less than two years!

But if our party had not had the strength it had, if it had not been so rooted, as we said it was, it would all have been over after June 1937 when the Stalinists made the party illegal. When all the press bodies censored and imprisoned most of our leaders. They slandered us in many ways.

Without the support of the people, who believed in our innocence, we would not have been able to do what we did or hide for so long. It was not enough, at that time, to be denounced but people knew us very well. The anarchists, the republicans and the socialists supported us. They helped us to not disappear altogether as the Stalinists would have liked.

ISABELLA: You're right. If the period of secrecy is not analysed there is no complete record of things. Let's go in order and start with the period of the civil war, or shortly before. What did you do? What responsibility did you have? What kind of political activity did you develop?

MARÍA: To answer you, I have to think back about sixty years to think about the history and memories of my life. I assure you it is not easy. I'll begin by clarifying for you that, before being part of the POUM which I joined in September 1935, I had already been, since 1929, an active member of the BOC, Maurín's party.

ISABELLA: As was Pilar Santiago.

MARÍA: Yes, like her. I was, at that time, sixteen years old. I was very young and politics was beginning to be part of my life. When, in 1935, the BOC merged with the Communist Left to form the POUM, I went through a period of political reflection, perhaps of crisis.

ISABELLA: Why?

MARÍA: I liked the Bloc (BOC), more than the POUM. I did not share Maurín's decision to create a party that was different from the one that already existed and which was very rooted and located in Catalonia. We liked the Bloc just the way it was and we didn't feel the need to join with people who had little in common with us.

ISABELLA: Do you mean the Trotskyists or those who had had a Trotskyist past?

MARÍA: I mean them. The Trotskyists, I didn't like them at all, to tell you the truth. I considered them sectarian and little different from the Stalinists. They were rigid, dogmatic, presumptuous and didn't know how to connect with people. They had no political power. We were forced to expel them from our party, due to political divergences. Subsequently, already in the middle of the civil war, it was Nin himself who wrote a letter, in which he said that supporters of the Fourth International could be in the POUM only in a personal capacity, not as a political group. Those who did not approve of this decision were expelled, because they were incompatible with the political line of the party. This was not a "painless" operation. It cost us a lot. It caused divisions, deep fractures, also inside us.

ISABELLA: Does your criticism also refer to characters like Nin or Andrade, who came from the IC[1] and had a Trotskyist political background?

MARÍA: No, I don't mean them. Nin adapted very well to a new situation, like others from the IC such as Iglesias, Gorkin, etc. We had problems only with those who wanted to apply Trotsky's theories to Spain. Trotsky had actively participated in the Bolshevik revolution and had created the Red Army but had not understood that Spain had a different culture and political tradition from that of Russia. We had our intellectuals and our theorists. Maurín was a man who guided us very well and we were very confident. We did not like the famous tactic of "entryism", which was designed, the Trotskyists argued, to penetrate inside socialist parties to "capture" their militants and "push" them to the left. To us, these sectarian practices did not appeal. We wanted to create a new party, that was in contact with the people, that was really independent of any external conditioning. We wanted to feel free to criticize everything and everyone: Stalin, Trotsky, and even Lenin. We didn't need bosses. If Trotsky wanted to create a party of his own he could have done so, but he would have had

---

1. Izquierda Comunista. A union of the POUM and el BOC (Bloque Obrero y Campesino). The leader of the BOC was Joaquin Maurín who was in prison for the duration of the war. For this reason both the POUM and the IC were headed by Andreu Nin.

to start from scratch. He could not lead a party that we had built from nothing, for years and years of work. For this reason we were forced to expel the Trotskyists from our party and not because we liked to throw people out. Rather the opposite. But they, with this logic of "entryism", they could also have divided our party and this we could not afford. The Trotskyists were dogmatic, sectarian and presumptuous

ISABELLA: What relationship did Nin and Maurín have?

MARÍA: Nin had been very close to Maurín because they had been active together in the CNT, in the anarchist movement. Nin was secretary of the International Red Trade Union and spent ten years in Moscow. There he came across Trotsky and his political way of thinking. After that he moved closer, politically, to us in the Bloc. In 1935 he created, with our party, the POUM. When Maurín was arrested at the beginning of the civil war, Nin was proposed as political secretary, not general secretary, of the party. We expected Maurín's release but that, unfortunately, did not happen. Nin had an important role in the party. A role that we would have never allowed him to have, if it were not because he had distanced himself, ideologically, from Trotskyist thought. I remember one day, years after the end of the civil war, that we met Maurín in Paris, where he sometimes travelled from the US for work commitments. He was in Paris for a conference on the war in Spain and on the POUM, in particular. He took the opportunity to come and visit me, Josep, my husband, Jordi Arquer, and others. I always remember him as a strong, generous, intelligent and cultured man. Men like that are really hard to find. I considered him a friend rather than a political leader. Josep had a lot of respect for him. While we were walking through the city we talked about the merge of the Bloc with the IC. Maurín knew very well that we didn't like that idea at all. We had to adapt to people we didn't like. We had a very precise political identity. Maurín confided to us that, more importantly than political reasons, it was his deep friendship with Nin that pushed him to merge with the IC. The IC was a very small party, concentrated mainly in Madrid and they had deep differences with us.

ISABELLA: What were those differences?

MARÍA: We of the Bloc were Catalan nationalists. We had as a priority the political, economic, and military independence of Catalonia. We wanted to speak our language again, vindicate our traditions and everything that, for centuries, the central government of Madrid had taken from us. All this, a Spaniard, even a Spanish comrade, can never understand. For us the revolution began in Catalonia and not in Spain! The Madrid government has never represented us. Those in Madrid have come to consider Basque, Catalan, and Galician as mere regional "dialects" and not true languages. They have tried to limit their use, prohibiting their spread. But people, both in universities and on the streets, have always spoken the language they have felt most to be their own. And in Catalonia the language that people speak is Catalan and not Spanish. For these reasons, at that time, there were profound differences with people in Madrid. On these issues, we had deep differences with the IC militants. We wanted a Catalan party, first of all. This political priority, a Madrid or Asturian militant, will never understand.

ISABELLA: I've been told a lot about Josep Rovira, the commander of the 29th Division. I have read many things about him. Everyone considered him a strong, straight, and brave man. A reference point for all militiamen. A man who instilled more respect than fear. And he was arrested and prosecuted like the other POUM militants. They dissolved their Division. I have read your statements to the court, included in the book *The Trial of the POUM* by Ignacio Iglesias. Any book that deals with the history of the civil war mentions his name and remembers him for the heroic actions carried out by his Division.

MARÍA: When Josep died, a biography was published[1] that dealt with his experiences during the civil war and the anti-fascist resistance. Josep's life had been very full. From a young age he had been exiled in France, in the twenties, for subversive political activity. He was arrested and prosecuted by the French government, with another group of friends, because he was organising an attack on the Spanish dictator Primo de Rivera. The entire radical French left, played its part. He was well aware that there was no "legal" method to overthrow the dictatorship. A very wide propaganda campaign was organised, which transformed that into a political process. They were sentenced to minimum penalties and were able to get out of jail quickly. But the dictatorship and the right-wing regime seemed eternal. And people did not have the strength to change the status quo. Josep went to Central America, to Guatemala.

---

1. Coll, Josep y Pané, Josep: Josep Rovira: una vida al servei de Catalunya i el socialisme, Ed. Ariel, Barcelona, 1978.

In 1931 he learned of the overthrow of the monarchy and the establishment of the Republic and that there was an amnesty for political prisoners. He returned in 1932 with the hope that some things could change. Over time he was disappointed. Josep was a revolutionary, not a bourgeois-democrat, and he thought that only the working class could truly discuss the political and economic pillars of constituted power. The working class would have had to bring down the secular power of the Catholic church, the army and the nobility. But people, at that time were not very aware of their strength. There was a world to build.

ISABELLA: Did you meet Josep when he returned from exile in 1932?

MARÍA: Yes, I met him in 1932 because we were both in the Bloc. But it was in 1936 when our story began.

ISABELLA: Were there other women in the POUM, in the Bloc, in the IC?

MARÍA: There weren't many but there were some. Most of them were women or the companions of party militants. Others were sisters or cousins. In any case, women were more numerous than in the other parties or movements and surely had more political awareness than the others. Also with the anarchists, there were women. But always less, compared to men.

ISABELLA: And you? Why were you in politics?

MARÍA: For ideological and sentimental reasons. I did not accept social injustice and wanted to fight for a better world. The social contradictions lived in my skin. My mother had been made a widow when she was young. She had four children and didn't really know what to do. The general economic situation was difficult, social contradictions were more acute than today. When I was a child there were many people who suffered from hunger and others who did not find work. Workers and their families lived very badly and began to organise in unions and fight to claim their rights. The conditions of the working class were not like the current ones.

ISABELLA: Victor Alba has told us several times that, during those years, the working class was more organised and more willing to fight the bosses. He could not lose anything other than his chains. Now, on the contrary, the workers have, in many cases, a petty-bourgeois mentality, and mobilise only to improve their economic conditions and not to demand political rights.

MARÍA: Víctor has written numerous books about the working class, Marxism in Catalonia, the reduction of working hours ... luckily we have a theoretician, among us, who writes and interprets what we ourselves do not have time to analyse, even if we live in our skin, all the contradictions of the planet.

ISABELLA: How many times a week did you go to the party headquarters?

MARÍA: Practically seven days out of seven. Every day, at night, when I finished work, I spent a little time with my colleagues. Being with them was, for me, a necessity and a pleasure.

ISABELLA: What did you do at the POUM headquarters?

MARÍA: We discussed everything; we analysed the political situation of the moment. We held meetings, assemblies, read books, magazines, newspapers ... When *La Batalla*[1] began to be published, we sold copies in the street. It was a pleasure to deliver the newspaper to the people for them to comment on everyday events. All this made me feel alive and a participant. If there was a need, which there always was, we went to the press and helped to fold the pages of the newspaper. In this way the party saved time and money. We did not have, at that time, automatic machines to fold the newspaper. Labour was needed, manual labour. We stayed there until three or four in the morning, and the next day we went to work. It was not like the kind of militancy there is now.

ISABELLA: I think you're quite critical about the current situation.

MARÍA: Yes, and I'll give you a concrete example. A few years ago I went to the headquarters of the Socialist Party in Barcelona, to discuss politics, and to do something, if necessary. It was a Saturday and I found it closed. It seemed odd. I saw a comrade and asked him why. He replied that it was a holiday and that was why they closed the party headquarters. I was stunned. When I militated, it was precisely on Saturdays and Sundays, when people did not work, when we dedicated ourselves, body and soul, to militancy. But things had changed and this was a sign of the times.

ISABELLA: Did the mentality of the people change a lot during the civil war? Did the small rules of social coexistence change?

---

1. POUM's weekly paper. It was crushed during the Stalinist coup in May 1937.

MARÍA: Yes, during the civil war, one could marry without difficulty. Any event could be done through civil ceremonies: births, weddings, burials. These ceremonies were lived collectively. The right to divorce had been obtained during the Second Republic. For abortion we had to wait until July 1936, in Catalonia, thanks also to the support of the secretary of our party, Andreu Nin, at that time minister of justice of the Generalitat. The Catholic Church lost much of its political power during the war.

My husband, in the front, officiated burials of many militiamen. And he also married many couples. These ceremonies regained their real meaning. People began, in that period, to want to radically change their lives and fight their own prejudices. This was the true Spanish revolution. It was a revolution made in homes, on the streets and in the workplace. Books have spoken little about what it meant for people to feel conscious, strong and the owner of their lives. For example, before I met Josep, I was married to another partner, but I wanted to feel free. I tore up my marriage certificate and considered myself disconnected from any previous emotional relationship. Josep and I got married years later, when we already had two children, and decided to do it for ourselves, not for others.

ISABELLA: In what year did your husband die?

MARÍA: In 1968 in Paris, a city in which we had decided to live, during our exile.

ISABELLA: Was he also arrested during the civil war?

MARÍA: Yes, several times. But the most serious thing that hurt him most, as a man and as a militant, was the dissolution of the militias. The end of that unique human, political, and military experience. I was at the front, with him, when he was told of the arrest warrant.

ISABELLA: Did you also participate in military actions in the militias?

MARÍA: Not directly. Some of us decided to and others did not. There were very few women at the front, four or five in all. We had many tasks both away from and at the front. There were so many things to do that we didn't have time to get bored. My husband was called to Barcelona in June 1937, when the Stalinists decided to dissolve our militias and arrest the leaders of the POUM. Many socialists and republicans were uncomfortable with the situation but were afraid to report it. They expressed, as best they could, their solidarity with us. The day after my husband was arrested, I went to the police department to learn about his state of health. The head of the department, with an indifferent air, told me that Josep had never arrived there, and that, rather, they were waiting for him so as to interrogate him. I started screaming with all my strength. "But how?" I replied, "if I accompanied him yesterday, right here! If I was with him at the front, when he was told that he should appear urgently in the police department of Barcelona!" And, always with an air of indifference, the police officer advised me to return the next day to see if Mr. Rovira had appeared there. And to think that my husband, a few days before, had received a telegram signed by the same head of the Aragon front, General Pozas. He congratulated Josep, as commander of the 29th Division, for a brilliant operation carried out with very little bloodshed and with the maximum results.

ISABELLA: In the book by Ignacio Iglesias, the full text of the telegram you are talking about is transcribed: "Arrived to my knowledge, brilliant behaviour of his forces, I am pleased to congratulate him, begging him to convey congratulations" [1]. ~Commander of the Northern constituency of the Aragon front.

MARÍA: General Pozas congratulated him on the successful action carried out in what is known as "Loma Milagros", at the front in Aragon, also evoked by Ken Loach in the film *Land and Freedom*. The one in which the priest who shot the militiamen is killed. Have you seen the film?

ISABELLA: Yes.

MARÍA: All the POUM militiamen, and my husband in particular, had respect for life and for human dignity. Josep always repeated that he had to avoid spilling blood uselessly. He did not want the war to make his militia turn to barbarism. For him the revolution began on the battlefield and it also manifested itself in respecting political prisoners.

ISABELLA: Is it true that there weren't many hierarchical differences between the commander and the other militiamen?

---

1. Andrés Suárez: El proceso contra el POUM. Un episodio de la revolución española, Ruedo Ibérico, Paris, 1974, page 89.

MARÍA: It's true. And I don't say it just because Josep was my husband. Everyone respected and esteemed him. They trusted him. Josep always asked the opinion of others, even in apparently irrelevant things.

ISABELLA: Did he complain, sometimes, about the lack of weapons and ammunition on the front?

MARÍA: Yes, always. It was a thing that affected him a lot. He said that the Stalinists had chosen the worst way to exert their political and military strength. Weapons and ammunition were missing on his section at the front. And militiamen were sometimes injured by their own weapons while firing at the enemy. His best weapons were those that they had managed to seize, fighting, from the fascists. On the front was also George Orwell, who was wounded in the throat, during a fight. When, after taking leave in Barcelona, he returned to the front, he was told that the POUM militias had been dissolved, and that the Stalinists were looking for everyone, him too. It was a miracle that he escaped arrest. When he returned to England, he wrote a beautiful book: "Homage to Catalonia", in which he speaks of life on the front and the lack of weapons rather than the political situation of Spain in 1936 or the problems with the Stalinists.

ISABELLA: What impressed me most about that book is how Orwell talks about the Spaniards. He does not hide some of their defects such as the lack of organisation and the inability to carry out their commitments. But Orwell argues that it is better to be a foreigner in Spain than in any other country in the world. People, in Spain, are generous, open, and altruistic.

Let's go back to the civil war and when your husband was in jail. Did you fear that the Stalinists could have killed him and that you would never see him again?

MARÍA: I could expect anything from the Stalinists, because they had already killed many of our militants and others were missing. Luckily, Josep was well known and the Stalinists could not have killed him without causing a scandal. The press and international public opinion called for his release. In addition, he, as commander of the army, could only be arrested by order of the military authorities, of the Minister of War in person. At that time, the minister was Indalecio Prieto, a socialist who didn't even know that my husband was in jail. Arresting Josep without notifying the minister had been imprudent. The Stalinists, formally so attached to the rules, had not respected the military code, something of no small importance, especially in times of war. Prieto was on our side and was informally informed that Josep had been arrested. The fact was scandalous! We managed to get in touch several times with Prieto and he was always very willing to try to help us. But the Stalinists had more control over events than the Spanish ministers and many times he himself felt helpless against the orders that came to him from above and which he simply had to obey. In spite of everything, he did everything possible to free Josep who, after 21 days in prison, was released. If my husband had not had someone to mobilise to obtain his release, he would have remained in jail during the entire period of the civil war, as happened to others less fortunate than him.

ISABELLA: Was he arrested in Barcelona?

MARÍA: At first, yes. But later he was transferred to Valencia. We managed to find out that he was there by chance, after much pressure from the police chief to obtain information.

ISABELLA: At that time there was an international campaign for the release of Nin.

MARÍA: Yes. We knew they were torturing Nin, but we couldn't get any more information about him! What the official authorities were telling us was contradictory: "We have never seen him, nor ever arrested him", and at the same time: "We are questioning him", "We cannot allow him to see anyone", "We cannot guarantee their safety", and, finally, the infamous lie that Nin had escaped thanks to the support of the fascist army! It was thanks to the international campaign of support for Nin, and the POUM militants, that the Stalinists could not kill others as they would have liked to do. Togliatti complained that the trial of the POUM had raised so much fuss and that most of the national and international press did not support their positions. Someone had rebelled against orders! The Pasionara was surprised that things had not gone as she expected, and the same "Pedro", who ran the PSUC[1] from La Pedrera in Barcelona, was really surprised that people believed the POUM militants more than them. Maybe it was for this reason that they didn't kill my husband. They could not afford an international campaign similar to the one with Nin. They already had too many dead bodies hidden in the closet.

1. Partido Socialista Unificado de Cataluña — Catalan Socialist Party

ISABELLA: They also arrested you, like Pilar Santiago?

MARÍA: No. I wasn't arrested and I don't know why. Pilar was jailed after her husband was murdered in the front. The Stalinists said he was a traitor and a fascist. The police did not give out any information. They said they didn't know where he was or what he had done. His case was already too uncomfortable. Pilar knew that the Stalinists had killed him at the front, shooting him in the back, accusing him of being a traitor and a fascist spy. Pilar was a very impulsive woman. Every day she went to see the high command of the police to ask for information about her husband and to claim at least his body. They treated her badly, implied that she was a bother and advised her to return quietly to her home. Pilar insulted them. She said that they were murderers, that they were the real fascists, covered up for by others and that they had murdered her husband at the front. Her husband was not a traitor, but a man who had fought for the freedom of his country. That is why she was arrested, as a "precaution", they said. Because she was dangerous, violent, and did not respect the military code. Because she committed crimes such as "prosecution offence" and other things. I don't know what the Stalinists expected people to do! Who would put up with murder and disappearance with calm and resignation? We saw our fellow detainees tortured and humiliated and we rebelled with all our strength against such things. No! We did not suffer in silence! Pilar was in jail for five months, simply for asking for information about her husband. An uncle of his, who was a deputy, managed to get her out of prison. She looked for a job in France, as a teacher. If she had stayed in Spain, she would have been arrested again because she did not stop protesting. Afterwards, Pilar decided to move to Mexico, and stayed there for many years, until she could officially return to Spain, after Franco's death in 1975.

ISABELLA: Let's go back to your husband, to Josep Rovira.

MARÍA: As I was telling you, thanks to Prieto's intervention, Josep was able to be saved. Prieto sent two telegrams to the director of the Valencia prison, who was a socialist, saying not only that he was to be released as soon as possible, but he was to be kept away from the Stalinists, who could have made an attempt on his life. In fact, the prison director behaved well with him, expressing his solidarity in various ways. When the time came for Josep to get out of jail, he feared there might be an attack on him. He could have waited in jail one more night, but he was in a hurry to get out. It was dawn, with poor visibility. The director illuminated the entire prison and there was so much light that it seemed like daylight. Two common prisoners accompanied Josep to a comrade's house, to protect him. But, after a short while, the three returned to jail.

ISABELLA: Josep was arrested again?

MARÍA: Yes. The legal proceedings against him were not very clear. The police considered his release inadmissible, an arbitrary act carried out by Prieto. They tried to arrest him again although they had no arrest warrant. He was in hiding for several months with the police looking for him, sleeping in friends' houses and escaping several times from our own house. But his father's house was very large and had three exits. Often, Josep escaped out the back when the police were about to enter through the front door.

ISABELLA: Did they never get to the point of arresting you, to catch him, as they did with other women like María Teresa Andrade and Luisa Gorkin?

MARÍA: No, they didn't. But they were often about to do so. In fact, in 1938, after several attempts, they succeeded in arresting Josep again, who went to prison in Valencia together with María Teresa Andrade, Arquer, his wife, and several others.

ISABELLA: During the underground period, what role did Josep play?

MARÍA: He dealt, like the others, with the trial, the party's underground press and several other things. The atmosphere was that of a witch hunt. Many lawyers who had to deal with the trial were threatened by the Stalinists and preferred to abandon the case. It was really hard to find someone who was willing to defend us. All these things my husband took care of with other colleagues.

ISABELLA: And when the war was over?

MARÍA: I had a 14-month-old girl and was expecting my second child. Josep was very worried about us. I was afraid that the fascists and the communists might kill us, for I spent most of my time asking for their release. The fascists were advancing and they were near Barcelona. The prisons were open but the director did not want problems with the

Stalinists and wanted to leave my husband and the other POUM militants in jail. I asked, along with other colleagues in the POUM, for the release of political detainees. Finally they yielded, less because of a sense of justice, than for fear that we would attack the jail and give them more problems than they already had.

The number of people on the left who were in jail was considerable: anarchists, communists, republicans ... There was a lot of confusion and I couldn't get in touch with Josep. I had left the city a few hours before him and had headed, with other companions, to the north, towards the border with France. I passed through Figueras and arrived near the border with France. I still didn't know anything about Josep. Suddenly, by chance, I heard a colleague telling me that he had met Commander Rovira the day before. "With Rovira?" I asked him, "And where is he now, Rovira? " "Yesterday I was in Figueras," was his response. I did not understand how I had not been able to see him because the day before, I myself had been there. The comrade explained that Josep had to hide from the Stalinists who were looking for him. They wanted to kill him and asked people if they knew where Rovira the "fascist" was. We were near the border with France and we left behind a defeated country, full of death, hunger, and misery. And the Stalinists still allowed themselves the luxury of looking for Rovira the "fascist"!

The Stalinists were a nasty piece of work. Sometimes, I met some of them in the streets of Barcelona. I got so angry that I felt like doing something. Anyway I have to say that, at that time, many people expressed their solidarity, in one way or another. The president of the Generalitat, Luis Companys, often contacted Josep, and other members of the POUM, to give us important information, allowing us to escape from the Stalinists. Companys was really an honest man, and he would surely have wanted to do much more for us if he had the chance to do so.

ISABELLA: I have read, several times, the speech that Companys delivered from the Generalitat of Catalonia, after the military coup on July 19th, 1936. On that occasion, Companys recognised that it had been anarchists, and revolutionaries of all kinds who had taken to the streets to fight fascism. It had not been the bourgeois parties, they had stood on the sidelines, waiting for the danger to pass. Companys said, on that occasion, that power belonged to the people and that it belonged to all those revolutionary organisations that had fought for freedom and democracy. But let's go back to your personal history, what happened when you crossed the border into France?

MARÍA: I went to northern France, to Brittany, with other POUM militants. Rovira went to Paris. He organised, with other partners, the anti-fascist resistance in France. He helped many militants to escape to other countries, to hide, or to find a job and to stay and live in France. He participated in military actions against the Nazis, organising many sabotages ...

ISABELLA: Did you also join the French resistance?

MARÍA: I couldn't because I had two young children. For this reason I returned to live in Spain, in Barcelona, at the home of Rovira's parents and looked after them because they were older.

ISABELLA: And in Spain, did you participate in the fight against the Franco regime?

MARÍA: Yes, of course, to the best of my ability. One day I was on la Calle Diagonal and a colleague told me the place and date of a clandestine meeting of the POUM in Barcelona. I went and returned to normal political activity. But in 1946 I returned to Paris to be able to live with Rovira until 1968, the year in which he died.

ISABELLA: Didn't you ever come back to Barcelona?

MARÍA: Yes, several times, clandestinely. Rovira risked a lot because there was always a warrant out for his arrest. We had no documentation and we had to cross the Pyrenees on foot, walking for days and days in the cold and the rain. Once we went to Barcelona when his father needed him, again when his mother was seriously ill. It was dangerous for us to stay in Spain. There were people who knew us and some could have denounced us.

ISABELLA: How did the news of the May events in Barcelona influence the morale of the militiamen?

MARÍA: As you could imagine. The news that arrived was confusing and dramatic at the same time. My husband could not understand how the Stalinists had been able to reach that extreme. The militiamen were baffled ... Some of them, three or four, along with other anarchist militants, decided to go to Barcelona to see what was happening. They reached Lleida and stayed there for a few hours. Then they immediately returned to the front. There was nothing else to do and they ran the risk of being shot by the Stalinists.

ISABELLA: As happened to several of them later.

MARÍA: Yes. Many militants and militiamen of the POUM were brutally detained and for no reason. It was enough not to agree with the ideology of the Stalinists to be considered an enemy, a fascist, and a provocateur. The war in Spain hides many horrors of this kind.

ISABELLA: Several POUM militants enlisted in the army hoping, in this way, to be safe from the Stalinists.

MARÍA: It was mistakenly thought that the army was a protected site. "They will not dare to attack us there," they said and believed. For everyone, even for those who considered us nostalgic extremists, it was clear that we were fighting the fascists. It was absurd for the Stalinists to kill and detain those who risked their lives fighting the fascists. But they reached this point.

ISABELLA: You told us that, in reality, things had developed differently than Ken Loach represented them in the film.

MARÍA: Yes, as I said before, my husband was not arrested at the front, but in Barcelona. Division 29, which he commanded, was dissolved little by little and not all at once. The Stalinists feared that the militia would rebel against them. For this reason they broke up the division before destroying it. Ken Loach has come to my house several times. He wanted to know everything about the front, about my husband, about the militiamen ... He told me that for cinematographic reasons he preferred to partially modify some things. A film does not necessarily have to describe reality. What matters is that its content is not altered. This is why Ken Loach chose not to give the division commander his real name and thus he was free to decide where and how the division was dissolved and also how his commander was arrested. A documentary that analyses, from a historical and political point of view, this period, is *Operation Nikolai*, made by Catalan television, which deals with the murder of Andreu Nin.

ISABELLA: We've seen it. They interview several POUM militants, including Víctor Alba, Solano, Nin's daughter, Teresa Carbó, etc.

MARÍA: Yes. Precisely, Teresa Carbó was the last person to see Nin alive. So she was able to testify, with absolute certainty, that he had been arrested. Nothing could have been clearer, but the Stalinists managed to deny even this. Teresa Carbó was a member of the POUM Red Aid, an organisation that offered medical assistance and moral support to the comrades that were in jail. She was well-known and that is why she could enter without any difficulty the place where he was being held. Teresa discovered, by chance, the presence of Nin. And he advised her to be cautious, so they wouldn't see her, because they could have arrested her. But Teresa was an impulsive woman, a brave militant, and often returned to look for Nin and to ask the competent authorities about his status. Then, and for this reason, they also arrested her. She caused too much trouble, they said, and she was too interested in Nin. For three months she was kept in jail, for "reasons of public order", for having seen something very uncomfortable.

The Stalinists did not want a woman to witness Nin's arrest. I could tell the press what I knew and they wanted to "solve" the Nin case without problems or complications. Teresa was imprisoned, with Pilar Santiago, for having seen too much and for not having wanted to obey orders. Now, Teresa, she's delicate, has eye problems. Too bad you can't see her. She was an exceptional militant.

ISABELLA: Salvador Clop is not well either. The day he had an appointment with us, last Monday, unfortunately he was admitted to hospital for a heart attack.

MARÍA: On the Nin case, I wanted to tell you that during the period of his detention, on the city walls, appeared written phrases such as: "Negrin Government, where is Nin?", And the Stalinists replied: "in Salamanca or in Berlin, with Franco or Hitler". In short, the Stalinists had no respect for anyone, not even for the dead. But history has proved us right. And that is what matters.

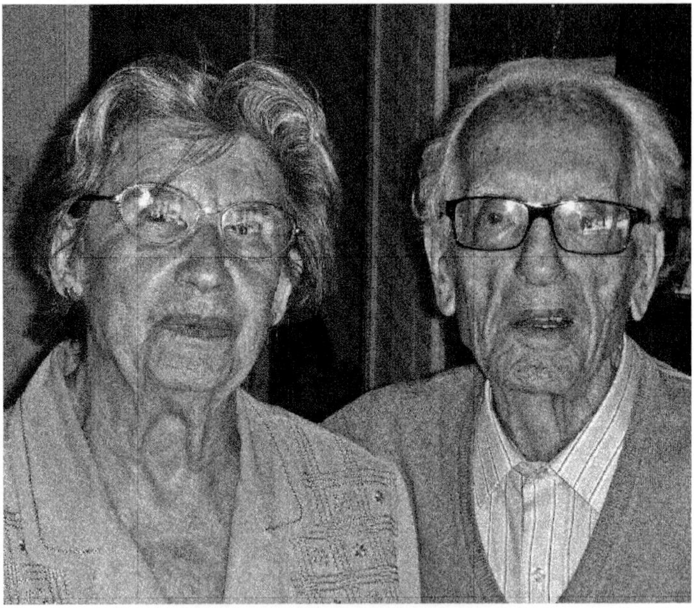

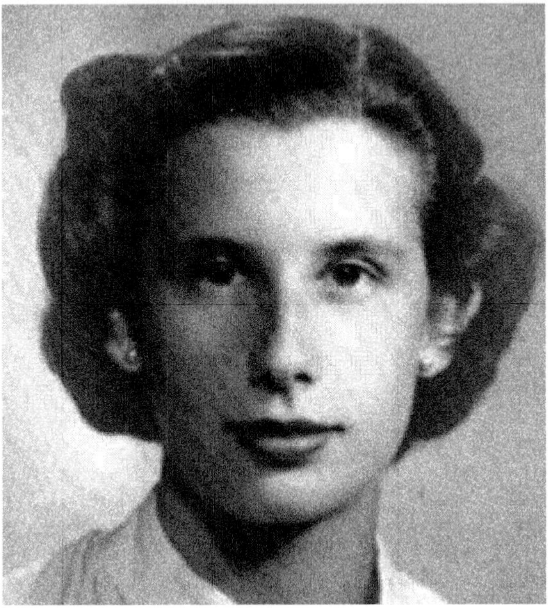

MARIA TERESA CARBONELL
POUM
Interviewed June 2010, Barcelona

Maria Teresa is president of the Andreu Nin Foundation in Barcelona. She witnessed the May Day events there and participated in the organisation of clandestine Marxist groups. She endeavoured to resume the publication of *Emancipación*, a feminist magazine, and record memories from all the POUM women. I organised many debates with her on Catalan, French, Russian and Italian feminism in Barcelona and Madrid.

ISABELLA: Hi Teresa. Can you tell me where and when you were born?

TERESA: I was born in Barcelona in August 1926.

ISABELLA: So you were very young during the civil war.

TERESA: Yes, I was just ten years old but I remember it clearly.

ISABELLA: Is there any special memory?

TERESA: During the Stalinist repression, my parents took several militants into our home including Solano and Roc.

ISABELLA: How long did they stay with you?

TERESA: They stayed with us for several months. This happened in 1937 when I was about eleven years old. Then I met Wilebaldo (Solano, her partner, see page 152) who is ten years older than me. Roc[1] also stayed with us for some time but eventually left because two wanted people shouldn't share the same shelter. It was too dangerous both for them and for us. Wile wrote articles for *Young Workers*, which was the newspaper of the Iberian Communist Youth. As children we regarded that situation as funny and exciting, albeit dangerous.

---

1. POUM fighter Joan Rocabert, who led a centuria during the war.

ISABELLA: What were your parents' names?

TERESA: My father was Joaquín Carbonell and my mother Luisa Cornejo. They were militants so we could host Wile, Roc, and other "subversives".

ISABELLA: Your parents were very brave, since they risked their lives and the lives of their children, too, for an idea.

TERESA: They were very well thought out. They would have been arrested if POUM members had been found in our house. Wilebaldo stayed with us for about eight months, but then the situation became complicated — we had security codes to enter our house, we were risking our lives and feared that a neighbour had denounced us. When the police came, Wilebaldo was no longer with us. Then he was arrested and my mother and I visited him in prison. She gave him food and letters and hid things for him.

ISABELLA: How did you learn that Wilebaldo had been arrested?

TERESA: We were in close contact with him and with other comrades.

ISABELLA: After the end of the war, did you stay in Barcelona or leave Spain?

TERESA: My parents considered this a lot but it was hard to move to another country with three children so we stayed in Barcelona. My father started work in a factory and we (three children) studied at the university.

ISABELLA: What did you study?

TERESA: Literature and philology at the university, but also French at a language school. Then I was granted a scholarship and went to Paris. There I met Wilebaldo and we fell in love.

ISABELLA: When did you meet in Paris?

TERESA: At the end of 1951. I liked living in Paris because I had left the Francoist regime behind. We could neither laugh nor read there. It was as if we had been locked up in a well. This is what a dictatorship looks like. In Paris, conversely, I could freely breathe.

ISABELLA: It was totally different, I guess.

TERESA: Yes, another world. I should have stayed there for only one year but I started a relationship with Wilebaldo and things changed. We got married in 1952 and I started working on my doctorate — everything turned out different to my expectations.

ISABELLA: The condition of women in Paris must have been completely different from Francoist Spain.

TERESA: It was very different. What is happening now in Spain is what I witnessed in France in the '50s. Recently, we have filled some gaps.

ISABELLA: Can you make yourself clear?

TERESA: At that time, women considered marriage the best way to solve their problems and although they studied, they were still looking for a husband instead of a job. If a woman didn't get married she stayed with her parents and if she had children and got married at a later time it was even worse. Workers couldn't save any money.

ISABELLA: Teresa, were you a POUM militant or a simple supporter?

TERESA: When I arrived in Paris, I was already a militant. In Spain, during the war, I was too young, but when I got married to Wilebaldo, I joined the party and became a militant.

ISABELLA: Did you attend meetings with the POUM militants in Paris?

TERESA: When I arrived in Paris I joined the militants whom I had known since I was a child. It was very exciting.

ISABELLA: Do you remember anybody in particular?

TERESA: I don't remember their names. Our social life was very active.

ISABELLA: Do you remember anything about the POUM female section?

TERESA: During the revolution, in Spain, a great movement of women rose up. They published a newspaper called *Emancipación* and a weekly magazine reporting the most important events. They emphasised the influence of the Catholic Church on women. These things may sound innocent today but were revolutionary at that time. For example, Pilar Santiago wrote that women shouldn't obey their husbands. Now it seems trivial but at the time this was a revolutionary idea.

ISABELLA: I met Pilar Santiago some time ago.

TERESA: Pilar was a skilful writer. Then there was Carlotta Dubany, who was the partner of Francesc de Cabo, one of the founders of the Nin Foundation.

ISABELLA: And there was also Teresa Rebull.

TERESA: Yes, but she was very young during the revolution, just like me. She wrote a book about her life which is full of interesting things. She also mentions her parents, who were anarchists and lived in Sabadell. Her life was really active. Then there was also Maria Manonelles, and Olivia Castelvi, who was a tailor like my mother and often visited us. The women on the female committee wrote on a notice board: from seven to eight, military education, then courses in politics. Some copies of the newspaper are kept at the national archives of Catalonia.

ISABELLA: In your opinion, at that time, were there any conflicts with regard to machismo among the party militants?

TERESA: No, there were no conflicts because at that time we all fought for the revolution. However, women started to organise themselves and this fact cannot be ignored. Later, during the exile, things were different. Nobody would have promoted groups of women only. Women had to work to make a living. Things were more complicated.

ISABELLA: During your exile, did you meet in Paris and in Barcelona?

TERESA: Yes, also in Barcelona. There was some POUM activity but it was very dangerous. Alberich[1], Rocabert, Quique[2], and others who had stayed in Spain during the Francoist regime also began to meet. When I moved to France I didn't follow events in Barcelona. Struggles were clandestine.

---

1. Manuel Alberich Olivé was a BOC and later POUM member who ran Barcelona's Lenin barracks until 1937.
2. Alias of Enrique Rodríguez Arroyo, a POUM militant jailed by the Communists and later Franco. On his release he fled Spain and served on the executive of POUM in exile.

ISABELLA: Do you remember anything about Nin's personal life? He had two wives, hadn't he?

TERESA: We met Cristina, who is the granddaughter of his first wife, and she told us that Nin had two children with his first wife, a boy and a girl. The boy was Cristina's father and she now lives in the Pyrenees.

ISABELLA: Yes, I know her, I just met and interviewed her.

TERESA: Whenever she comes to Barcelona she always visits us and asks Wilebaldo about her grandfather. She's a very nice girl.

ISABELLA: Are you in contact with Silvia, the other granddaughter of Nin?

TERESA: No, only with Cristina. She went to London and they met there, it must have been very exciting. And then there was Nora, Silvia's mother, who is the daughter of Nin and Olga, his Russian wife. Nora was the youngest, while the elder is Ida and lives in the United States. She has children but never comes here. Nora is a few years younger than me and I invited her to Paris, but she prefers going to London to visit her daughter. If she came to Barcelona, I would really like to meet her.

ISABELLA: Although you were young, do you remember any anecdotes about the Stalinists?

TERESA: Actually we were barely in contact with them, but I remember Salvador Roca, a journalist who was our neighbour. In short, he became a PSUC member but he helped us whenever he could. He invited us to dinner and behaved fairly with us although he was one of them.

ISABELLA: A positive anecdote.

TERESA: I believe that he became a Stalinist only for his own interests. After the war, he went to France, stayed in a camp and died. We loved him very much. We treated him as a family member.

ISABELLA: What were you saying before?

TERESA: Yes, I remember that the POUM women decided to wear a blue shirt as a sign of recognition. They wanted to share even the same clothing.

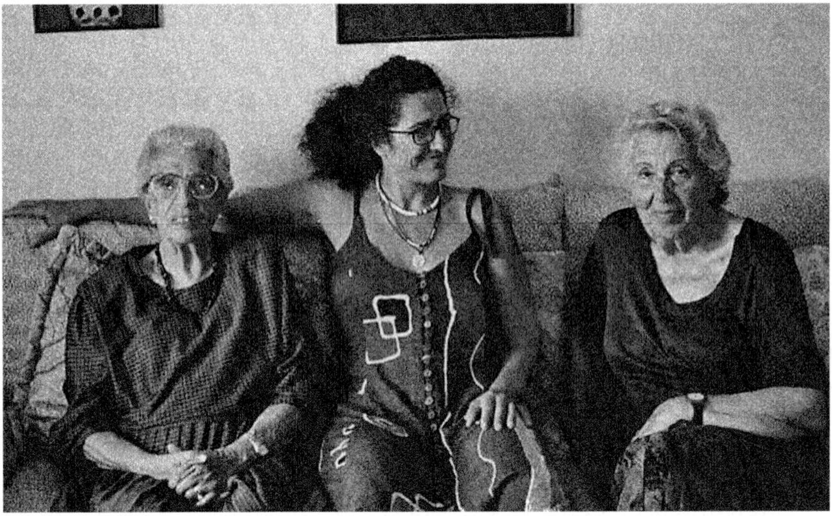

Pilar Santiago
(1914-1998)
POUM | Interviewed June 1996, in Barcelona

Historians with a Marxist background interpret traditional historiography as the work of the ruling social classes and they counter it with a history written from the perspective of the oppressed classes and, in particular, the working class. In fact, until the surge of the second wave of the feminist movement in the 1970s and the dedication of female historians to the question of women in history the presence of women was hardly reflected in the process of history.
~ **Mary Nash**
Women and the Workers' Movement in Spain 1931-1939

"They came from different countries: from Italy, Norway, Holland and Bulgaria. They couldn't talk to each other. They had no common language. But together they sang The International".
~ **Ilya Ehrenburg**
Correspondent in the Spanish Civil War

Santiago was born in Barruelo (Palencia) in 1916 and died in Barcelona in 1998. She was a practicing political feminist and opposed the kind of sexual discrimination which led many women to abandon social and political activity and cut themselves off in their private lives. Interviewed several times by the Irish historian Mary Nash, when producing the book *Women and the Workers' Movement in Spain*, she was well aware that only a feminist revolution would be able to bring to an end in a radical manner the existing patriarchal power structure.

She was detained in 1937 by the Stalinists on a charge of insulting the Public Prosecutor since she had repeatedly asked for information about her husband, Juan Hervás, a POUM militant who was shot at the front, and she spent several months in a republican prison. She refused to accept the official police version of events and maintained her husband had never drawn swastikas nor had collaborated with the enemy. She was convinced her husband had been shot because of his politics.

In prison she met other women and militant sisters. Amongst these were Teresa Carbó, Maria Teresa Andrade, and Luis Gorkin. At the end of the

Spanish Civil War, Pilar moved to Mexico. She returned to Catalunya after the death of Franco in 1975.

She worked on the production of the film Land and Freedom and analysed, along with the director Ken Loach, the themes of which related to the condition of women during the Spanish Civil War. The last years of her life saw her spending time in Barcelona and Mexico City.

PILAR: I know you have interviewed Ignacio Iglesias.[1]

EVA: Yes. We met him a few days ago in Vilanova, a little town near the sea, on the Costa Brava, He now lives in Paris and was only in Barcelona for a few days.

PILAR: I hear his health is none too good.

ISABELLA: Yes. He has difficulty talking. But he is very active, intelligent, kind, and has a good sense of humour. He even joked about his state of health. Our meeting with him, as with all of you members of POUM, has been a really enriching experience. Not just from a political point of view but also from a human and cultural perspective.

PILAR: I completely understand where you are coming from. It is the difference which exists between those who interpret history in books and those who live it in the first person; those who analyse events and those who investigate them.

ISABELLA: Talking to you all, not only do I become aware of aspects which the history books overlook, but also the very way the facts are told — giving them life and meaning.

PILAR: We lived through a special historical period. A period in which every political event had influence on our private life. It made you realise that some things were a result of a long historical and political process which involves all of us at some level.

---

1. Ignacio Iglesias Suárez was made leader of POUM's Libertarian Youth in 1935, fought in the war and was a political editor of *La Batalla*, POUM's weekly newspaper before fleeing to exile in France after the war. He remained a POUM activist in exile until 1953, working as a journalist and translator until his retirement in 1973. He died in 2005.

EVA: Are you talking about POUM?

PILAR: Not only. I am thinking of all the radical left: socialists, republicans, Trotskyists, anarchists...

ISABELLA: The anarchists were an impressive, political force in Spain during the Civil War.

PILAR: The anarchists were involved in all areas of society and production in the country. They were serious organised militants. To all of them I would offer my admiration and recognition of what they did.

ISABELLA: For what reason?

PILAR: For their strength and consistency. I have known hundreds of anarchist families in Catalonia. I have been able to see how they educated their children and how the men related to the women. They accepted no compromise of any kind with the system. For them the revolution began at home, in the factory and in the town. They didn't baptise their children and they didn't impose any ideology on them. These things may seem trivial to you but they are not. How many people are really ready to organise their lives and those of their children in order to perpetuate their faith and ideals in which they believe? In contrast with the collective silence and general conformity they stood out because they questioned their private lives and their day to day existence. And then they also organised their struggles in the workplace, they led strikes and protested on the streets. For me the anarchists had something more, something the rest of us lacked.

ISABELLA: So why did you join the POUM and not the anarchist groups?

PILAR: Because I felt closer to the POUM than the anarchists politically. I'll say this, in those days the fact is that none of us knew what it really meant to call yourself a communist, a Marxist, or simply a revolutionary. In Spain the workers were more familiar with Bakunin's *Anarchy and The State* than *Das Kapital* by Marx. We faced up, for the first time, to the challenge of studying difficult books on economics, history and politics, and we asked ourselves about the real meaning of some of the terms used.

ISABELLA: For example?

PILAR: We would ask ourselves what the term 'added value' meant. To help ourselves we came up with a real-life example. We would say: if the capitalist earned 10 and gave the worker two, that meant that he kept the other eight, and the capitalist earned those eight thanks to the labour of the worker. This work was an exploitation because the worker had the right to manage the means of production along with other workers. The working classes lived in dismal conditions. There was no right to retirement, medical assistance, unemployment insurance. They earned just enough to survive. The capitalist on the other hand got ever richer. The money that he could save served for other investments and allowed him to live a far better life than us. Workers have to organise, fight for their rights, stop production, show their strength to the boss class, and society at large.

I am just outlining for you the sense of our discussions. We had begun to elaborate theoretical analysis of the history of the working class movement. All of us, in fact, were very well aware of what we were doing and we were very keen to keep working on these themes.

ISABELLA: The conditions lived by the working classes at the beginning of the century are not comparable to those of today.

PILAR: In those days, life was hard for working people and their working conditions were even worse. They had no rights of any kind and there were no laws to protect them. You could be sacked for any reason, even for very stupid reasons: because you were ill, because you attended union meetings, etc. The fight between capitalists and workers was in deadly earnest. People lived in constant fear of killings, reprisals, arbitrary violence, and arrest. This struggle came to a head in such a way, in Spain, that it led almost without people noticing, to Civil War in July 1936. People think of that date as being the start of hostilities but the violent political and social tension had already been there for at least a couple of decades.

Spain had lived through the unsuccessful republican experience in 1931. But at that time, people were scared of being too radical and carrying through political and economic reforms which would upset the political right. The left wing coalition which won the first elections ended up revealing itself as too moderate and incapable, which guaranteed a certain continuity with the previous regime. This first Republican government lasted till 1933, the year new elections were called which were won by the coalition of the centre right, led by Gil Robles. This was known as the 'black two years' during which timid attempts at reform in agriculture, education, and fiscal policy, along with the relationship with the Catholic Church, were buried for good.

In 1934 a revolt broke out in Asturias which involved the most radical and politically aware sections of the working classes. They made many demands of both an economic and political nature. Repression was violent. The government used north African troops alongside all the forces of law and order at its disposal. Those who were killed, injured, or who disappeared, numbered in the thousands. All the others involved were subject to mass arrest, accused of taking up arms and insurrection. The Asturian revolution will never be erased from the collective memory of the Spanish proletariat. As a result of the barbaric repression in Asturias, the reactionary government of Gil Robles suffered serious strains within itself which brought about, in 1935, the dissolution of the Congress, and, in February 1936, there were new elections. The workers' movement, this time without the anarchists calling for an abstention, voted unanimously for the Popular Front.

ISABELLA: Those elections also gave rise to difficult political decisions.

PILAR: Most certainly. As I was saying, the anarchists were very consistent and faithful to their ideals. During the elections of April 1936 they decided to vote solely in order to liberate their comrades in prison and for nothing else.

ISABELLA: You mean to say they had no faith in the bourgeois institutions?

PILAR: The anarchists gave no credit to the state's institutions. They rejected parliamentary politics, party politics, political compromise, and political agreements. They were critical of the politics of those who had already renounced political activity and who only wanted a seat in government. How not to agree with them?

ISABELLA: You were telling us that before civil war broke out the political situation was quite tense.

PILAR: Yes, when the left won the elections in February 1936, the right began to organise itself and prepare for a coup.

ISABELLA: One of the main accusations made by the right of the left was that the elections were a fraud and that they should be rerun.

PILAR: The fascists could not understand how the people, in Spain, could vote for the left. That people that they had bought, humiliated, and subjugated had decided to vote against them. For them this was inconceivable. The outcome of the elections had to have been, according to them, manipulated.

ISABELLA: They said, amongst other things, that the majority political system did not guarantee a perfect reflection of the votes cast in the parliamentary distribution of seats.[1]

PILAR: How ridiculous! They were trying to create a problem that didn't exist! But they were forgetting the fact that they themselves had called for the electoral system and that in 1933 the same system was in place when the right had won.

The truth is that, for fascists, voting is just a formality. For them it is for those that hold power to wield it, or whosoever could seize it by force. fascists are always associates of the strongest, the usurpers, and those with the most power. They control the military, finance, politics, religion. They know very well that to in order to crush the weaker social classes they need to be united, organised, and strong.

ISABELLA: In April 1936 they went into the elections divided.

PILAR: Yes, politically, they were divided. But they were united militarily and got organised a few months later thanks to the support of European fascist powers.

ISABELLA: Why did the military coup begin in Morocco?

PILAR: Because Morocco, at that time, was a Spanish-French colony. It was a military training field for the colonial powers. Paradoxically they used North African troops to put down the Asturian revolution and later they were used as shock troops in the anti-republican coup.

ISABELLA: There was a great debate because the Republican government did not support a campaign for political independence in Morocco. Only in

---

1. The Republic's electoral rules established a mixed system with both majority voting and proportional representation with open lists which set aside 20% of the parliamentary seats for minority candidates in every electoral district. The outcome of this system in the elections of February 1936 was that, with very little difference in the number of votes cast, the left returned a significantly larger number of deputies than the right (278 as opposed to 136 out of a total of 473)

that way could they have given support to the most militant sectors of the workers' movement. The Moroccan troops would have been able to rebel against the greater Francoist state. Only by gaining their own independence and freedom, would they have fought the Spanish usurpers. It didn't happen. Officially they did nothing to support Moroccan independence.[1] The Republican government was on the defensive even before war broke out.

PILAR: Yes. The Republican government responded in a very timid fashion to the fascist threats. Our dear governors didn't know how to react. They didn't want to hand arms out to the people. They didn't want to start a social revolution. They hoped that, somehow, the fascists would quietly go away without demanding any change!

ISABELLA: But the question of Morocco?

PILAR: What the politicians really didn't want was to provoke the other European sates who they hoped in some way would help 'free' and 'democratic' Spain. It was in the name of this European loyalty that they did not support the struggle for independence in Morocco. They could not bring themselves to believe that a rebellion in the Moroccan colonies would have been able to cause problems in the Francoist camp. They didn't want to interfere with the interests of countries like France or England. Countries which, in any case, didn't lift a finger to save the Spanish Republic. A sad story.

ISABELLA: The Republican front also had internal divisions.

PILAR: The Republican front was divided internally more than ever. Our objectives were different, as also was our political vision. We in POUM as a political group felt much closer to the anarchists.

ISABELLA: How so?

PILAR: We were fighting for a revolution. We believed in social change. We wanted a country that was free and democratic in which the working classes would hold power. We wanted to collectivise the land, the factories. We wanted women to play an important role in society.

---

1. Abel Paz wrote on this subject in *The Moroccan Question and the Spanish Republic*

ISABELLA: It was those factors which differentiated you from the Stalinists?

PILAR: We were completely different from the Stalinists and we soon realised this. Before the war broke out we began publishing in our papers news about what was happening in the Soviet Union. These news articles had a great effect on us. We knew that in the country of socialism there were terrible purges aimed at eliminating physically and politically the main agents in the Russian revolution! We asked ourselves: How is it possible that Trotsky, Bukharin, and other Soviet leaders could be accused of betraying the Soviet Union? How was it possible that Stalin's power had brought this about? We published a lot of information in *La Batalla* about the political situation in the Soviet Union. We immediately positioned ourselves against Stalinism and that wasn't easy.

ISABELLA: In what way?

PILAR: In the sense that many of us, then as well as now, were communists, which meant we were guilty for whatever happened anywhere in the world. For many being a communist and being a Stalinist were the same thing. They were not able to see the differences that existed between us.

ISABELLA: That is also why, often, people have confused and simplified the events that took place in Barcelona in 1937 as simply a struggle between factions.

PILAR: Yes there have been those who have held to that theory. Most people were not even made aware at the most basic level about the facts. I have been lucky enough to have been born into a family that knew what it wanted and was aware of what was happening. My father was a traditional socialist. A very serious and honest man. I remember him being very critical of the Catholic church and he didn't want us to be with priests and nuns. If it had been up to him, we would not have been baptised. But my mother insisted, if only so we would not be discriminated against. But he taught us to be critical of established power. My father was always on the side of the poor and always defended the interests of those who didn't have the means to defend themselves and fight back. He was the director of the Ateneo Popular and when a worker died, he helped with the funeral and supported the family. But when the coffin arrived at the church he remained outside. He didn't want to live out his grief inside a religious institution he didn't like. In those days there were hired mourners at funerals. I used to wonder how it was possible that people could cry in exchange for money.

ISABELLA: What were the Ateneos Populares?

PILAR: They were the first political and educational experiment to help the public access a culture they were alienated from. They organised classes in literacy, dance, theatre, music, art ... It was perhaps the first and somewhat naïve attempt by the workers to take some political power. You need to realise that in those days schools were in the hands of the priests and nuns, who did not hand down a critical or complete sense of culture. The Ateneos Populares started out at the beginning of the 19th century and, as a political experiment, they still exist today.

ISABELLA: You were talking about your family.

PILAR: In my family we were heavily involved in the political events inside the country. My aunt, for example, gave lodging, for several months, to a young anarchist who had taken part in a shooting. Unfortunately this lad was arrested and this hurt us a lot. My uncle Crescenciano Bilbao[1], my mother's brother, was a very serious, militant socialist, one of those who was uncomfortable living in a consumer society. When he was young he was persecuted on several occasions by the police for his political beliefs. He hid in the mountains and my mother took food to him. After that he succeeded in becoming deputy for the PSOE for the duration of the Civil War. It was thanks to him that I survived my detention.

ISABELLA: When were you arrested?

PILAR: I was arrested during the summer of 1937 during the repression implemented by the Stalinists against our party.

ISABELLA: Were you actively involved in the political activity of POUM?

PILAR: Yes, I was directly involved in the political life of the party and I did all that I could as a militant. I would distribute issues of our journal, I attended political meetings, I wrote political articles. I was invited several times along with Nin to give talks about positions held by the party. I was quite active but that wasn't why they detained me...

---

1. Crescenciano Bilbao (1892-1961) was a miner and a key member of the PSOE (Socialist Party) and the UGT (Socialist trade union), a follower of Prieto. A deputy for Huelva during the civil war, he later became general subcommisioner for war.

ISABELLA: What was the reason?

PILAR: The Stalinists shot my husband at the front. I was constantly protesting to the military authorities, asking for news of his whereabouts. And they told me my husband was a fascist and a traitor and that they had had to shoot him whilst he was attempting to cross over to enemy lines. They thought I would be satisfied with such an absurd version of events. I knew that everything they told me was a lie. I knew my husband was a communist, a militant with the POUM and that he had never thought, even remotely, of passing over to the enemy. I also knew that Nin, Andrade, Gorkin, Solano, Rovira, and all the other members of POUM who were shot or arrested were neither fascists nor traitors. I knew these people well. I had carried out political activities with them for years. I had shared with them the good times and the bad, the stresses, and the fear. The official versions convinced me of nothing. I protested and I fought back. What else could I have done? Give up? I felt crushed and I was never to see my husband again.

ISABELLA: Tell us about him?

PILAR: His name was Juan Hervás. I had met him when I was 18 years old, in the school where both of us taught. The head was from Lérida and his name was Victor Colomer[1] and he was like us an activist in Bloc. So began the story of our love for each other and our political evolution. One year later, Juan and I were married. Juan was a serious and educated activist. It couldn't be said that he was an extremist. We were very good friends with Maurín. He also taught, like us, in the school at Lérida. When the war began he went to fight at the front. Several times I went to see him and I was surprised at how they managed to survive in such precarious conditions as those they were facing. There were shortages of everything: bread and water, sleep and rest. The political situation was becoming ever more tense both in the towns and on the battlefields. The Stalinists would call us traitors, fascists and members of Franco's fifth column. How was it that they were able to say such things of us? How could they dare slander us so openly?

---

1. Victor Colomer (1896-1960) was a teacher and companion of Maurín all the way through his political and professional life. He left the BOC when the later joined up with the IC in order to form POUM. During the Civil War he was part of the leadership of the PSUC from which he was expelled in 1939 accused of Trotskyism. Exiled in Mexico he became involved with the Catalan Socialist Movement. Recently, Ferrán Aisa had published an interesting book about his life and that of Maurín: El laberint roig: Victor Colomer I Joaquím Maurín, mestres I revolucionaris, Pagès editors, Lleida, 2005

ISABELLA: They had the powers that be on their side. The power of a state which had forgotten the lessons of its own revolution. Added to that was the fact that the Soviets were the only ones who were supplying the Republican government with arms, because the other governments had declared themselves 'neutral' during the Spanish conflict.

EVA: Not forgetting that Italy and Germany continued supplying, non-stop, arms and munitions to Franco's army under the noses of the European great powers who pretended not to know what was going on.

ISABELLA: Coming back to the situation in Spain in May 1937. Tell us your own story.

PILAR: I remember those terrible days in May. I stayed at home, terrified, hoping that the situation would calm down. The political situation had grown more tense and we all feared for our lives. Suddenly the worst happened. When the fighting stopped, all the blame was laid on us, we who were most critical of Stalinist politics. The fact that we were, numerically, a smaller force than the anarchists made us very vulnerable. If the Stalinists had directly attacked the anarchists they would have paid heavily for their stupidity.

ISABELLA: But the anarchists supported you in your fight against the Stalinists.

PILAR: They gave us their support in an exemplary fashion. They supported our theories and our arguments. And from a practical point of view they helped many of us escape and survive in clandestinity. The very same anarchists, especially Federica Montseny, continually called for the release of POUM militants. Thanks to their support we were not condemned as traitors by the Special Tribunal for Espionage and High Treason, set up in 'our honour'. We were condemned as revolutionaries, as those who had dared remain on the barricades, in order to defend the rights of the working class in May 1937.

In those days there was a lot more fear and we believed that something terrible might happen to us. And hardly a month had gone by since they had told me of the shooting of my husband at the front. I didn't have the strength to stay calm and so every day I went to the Council for Public Order who had responsibility for the police. I would speak to some bureaucrat or other who simply repeated the official version: that my husband was a traitor, that he had been shot in the back whilst trying to escape in order to make contact with the fascists. To give weight to their version of events I was told that he hadn't been alone and that other party members had tried to cross over to the fascist lines. I knew these comrades well and that at no time would they have gone insane and start drawing swastikas and throwing the fascist salute with their arm in the air. The police administrators could say what they liked. I knew those men well and, above all, I knew my husband, Juan[1].

I carried on bothering the military authorities. I wanted, at least, to have my companion's body returned. They got mad at my constant questioning. They realised I might do something unwanted. That in contrast to my hard, strong and powerful words theirs lost all meaning. That is why they arrested me.

ISABELLA: How long were you imprisoned?

PILAR: About six months. Months of anguish and despair during which the pain of having lost Juan added to my incarceration. By luck, the governor of the prison was a very understanding woman and she tried, in every way, to help us live out those months with some peace and calm.

ISABELLA: Did you know any other women who were detained in the prison?

PILAR: Yes, with me were Maria Teresa Andrade and Teresa Carbó. Teresa Carbó was imprisoned as a consequence of Nin's detention. She had been to see Nin in prison and had spoken to him the day he was arrested. But, quite suddenly, Nin disappeared and the Stalinists gave contradictory versions of events: they had never detained him; yes, we did detain him but he has been released; he was in contact with Franco's fifth column; the fascists came and liberated him; no we never tortured him. A so it went on with various contradictory explanations. The fact that Teresa had spoken with Nin on June 16th 1937 was in stark contrast to all their versions of events. They arrested her so she couldn't spread 'her' version of the truth; which happened to be 'the' truth.

ISABELLA: What type of person was Teresa Carbó?

---

1. He was shot along with Joan Hervàs and the POUM member Jaume Tepat and the CNT member José Meca, the latter a political commissary of the 141 brigade which was part of the 32nd division led by the Communist Eduardo Barceló. The three who were shot belonged to a transportations company that was heading for the front in Huesca

PILAR: She was an exceptional woman, a really incredible activist. She was part of the POUM's Red Aid and was in contact with all our political prisoners who were rotting in the republican prisons. She tried to console them and give them some human comfort. They all loved her very much. She was a model of strength and courage. Unfortunately she is not very well right now. She has problems with her eyes. But if you had known her at that time she would have fascinated you.

Nin, when he saw her, advised her to be very careful because he feared something serious might happen to her and they might have been able to implicate her in the repression. But Teresa paid no attention to these warnings. Several times she asked for news of Nin. She wanted to know where they had arrested him and that was an inconvenient question.

ISABELLA: Teresa paid a heavy price since they arrested her as well.

PILAR: We knew very well that if we kept our mouths shut we would not have been arrested. If I had said, "ah, my husband was a fascist, a traitor", they wouldn't have come looking for me. They would have consoled me as they consoled the fascists' wives. But the truth was very different as everyone knew very well! Nin was arrested! They had murdered my husband! They could deprive us of everything except the memories we had of those we loved.

ISABELLA: What were you accused of when you were detained?

PILAR: I was detained for offences against government officialdom because I persistently asked for information about Juan but also because I insulted all those who threw mud at his name. I called them hypocrites, murderers, cowards, traitors, and false communists. All those words bothered them. They hoped for our resignation and silence but we responded with pride and courage. That is why they decided to lock me up in order to shut me up. They came to my home to arrest me and treated me as a terrorist and a murderer.

Teresa Carbó, on the other hand, was detained for slander. They had the cheek to say that she had views and she only sought to defame the republican police. And they decided to lock her up. The Stalinists were really treacherous people. They were callous and stupid in the service of Russian communism. At that time I became embarrassed for having read with some passion over the previous years, pages and pages about the Russian revolution, the exaltation of the party, the proletarian victory.

I asked myself what had happened to all those things that had motivated the workers all around the world. Certainly it wasn't on the faces and in the hearts of those who came to arrest me that day. Nor those who knocked on the doors of Teresa Carbó, Luisa Gorkin, Maria Teresa Andrade, and many other revolutionary men and women. I have in mind right now something strange that happened.

EVA: What is that?

PILAR: Some years ago a man, whose name I don't remember, called Maria Manonelles. He told her he was on the point of dying and he wanted to speak to someone in the POUM. Maria and Victor Alba went to see him. He told them that during the Civil War, he had been directed by the Stalinists to do the job of sending radio messages in which he said he was a the POUM activist and wanted to make contact with the fascists. He was near death and didn't want to take his shame with him. He wanted to be forgiven by us. This episode is really incredible. It shows how they all, many years later and however they could, regretted their actions and wanted to 'put the record straight' even though they were not all able to do so. These people trouble me because I think we also need them so we can die in peace. After having tried to kill us, one after the other without pity.

ISABELLA: Now they have opened up a number of Soviet archives and many truths have come to light.

PILAR: Many truths that we have known for a long time and which we have been forced to run away from. Stories of death and suffering.

ISABELLA: Coming back to your personal story. After several months in jail they managed to get you out.

PILAR: Yes, thanks to my uncle's intervention, the Socialist deputy we were talking about earlier. He found me work in Lyon as a primary school teacher. I managed to escape clandestinely with false documents and I was able to start a new life. After a few years in Paris, I met the man who was to be my second husband[1].

---

1. This was doctor Rafael Trueta, the brother of Dr. Josep Trueta, famous for having introduced a new and effective way of treating war fractures during the conflict.

ISABELLA: Was he also with the POUM?

PILAR: No. He was with the Catalan Republican Cavalry. He was more moderate than me. In 1941, together, we left France. He was a doctor and wanted to go and live in Uganda to save children who were dying of hunger. But, like many other Spaniards, we went to Mexico to Veracruz.

ISABELLA: What was your life like in Mexico?

PILAR: It was very quiet and very happy. The Mexican President, Cárdenas, had welcomed a large number of Spanish exiles. He was a very good and intelligent man who allowed us the opportunity to get back to living a proper life. I taught and my husband continued working as a doctor. All was good for us and we asked for nothing.

ISABELLA: After many years you came back to Spain.

PILAR: I think a have a very strong tie to my country. To leave the place where you were born is not easy for anyone. Here, for example, I had my parents.

ISABELLA: They didn't want to escape?

PILAR: No, they wanted to carry on living in Spain where they had always lived. During the Franco regime they fell ill and I made an official request to return so I could be with them, even if only for a short time. But Franco's government refused and I learnt of their deaths by telephone which made it feel very impersonal. The absurd Falangist military regime had deeply affected my personal life. They had destroyed my hopes.

ISABELLA: I would like to ask you about the status of women during the period of the Civil War. I know that Mary Nash has interviewed you a number of times whilst writing her book Defying Male Civilization: Women in the Spanish Civil War.

PILAR: Yes. What she was interested in, above all, was the status of women within moderate and radical left wing political organisations. What comes to light is a really distressing picture. As they say: revolutionaries on the outside and reactionaries on the inside. Many comrades thought that the gender difference simply didn't exist or that if it did exist it was not as important as class issues. They would reduce our feminist demands to the simple economic dimension. For them a rise in income would have solved all our existential problems. They had heard nothing of what we wanted and of the potentialities we were expressing.

ISABELLA: It was the classic logic, common to Marxist thought, a 'revolution in two times'. One revolution that, once carried out, would resolve all the existential problems of all the political minorities, meaning any group that didn't have social power.

PILAR: For Marxists, the revolution was going to solve everything. It would solve the gender question, class, race ... It was enough to see what had happened in the countries in Eastern Europe. There women had won the right to abortion, divorce, dignity in the workplace. But when they got home, they had to look after the kids and put food on the table. Men retained political power and were not willing to relinquish it.

ISABELLA: During the Civil War what were the women's groups like?

PILAR: There were different types. There were women's groups which were in perfect alignment with the party-political line and didn't think it was either the right time, nor necessary, to seek conflict with the masculine elements of the group.

They would say: men and women, at that historic time, were fighting for the same objectives. Our struggle was indivisible. There were other groups we might call feminist, although in those days nobody talked of feminism, who were fighting for specifically women-related demands. These groups were in conflict with male power. The most important of these groups was Mujeres Libres[1] which found its inspiration, more or less, in anarchist ideas[2].

These women had great courage when it came to claiming their rights, often going head on in conflict with the most radical sectors of the

---

2. Sara Berenguer: 'Come nacque l'aggruppazione Mujeres Libres', pp 63-64 as quoted in Chi c'era racconta. La rivoluzione libertaria nella Spagna del 1936, Zero in Condotta Edizioni, Milano, 1996:, 'These sisters, at their meetings, would talk about organisation and libertarian communism... It was in the ongoing struggle that these women found strength... The situation made these women feel solidarity for each other and while they helped with union meetings they had an agreement that one of them, in strict rotation, would look after the children of the others so the mothers could get away something which gave them a certain freedom of action... Women in this way showed with the strength of their will the rich potential they had...'

Spanish revolutionary movement. Telling a member of the militia who was manning the barricades that when he got home he had to help his wife in the kitchen and he had to look after the children wasn't the easiest thing in the world. It was interesting to see how these comrades who wanted to change the world in practice didn't want, in any measure whatsoever, to question their private life.

EVA: Our comrades are forever falling into that trap! They can say what they like about the capitalist system: that it is unjust, cruel, mean ... but for them the patriarchal system makes them all starry eyed because it puts them in a privileged position which, obviously, they don't want to give up too easily.

ISABELLA: In fact, when women organise themselves independently, they are seen to be sectarian and unready to fight for the real proletarian revolution.

PILAR: Men don't realise how they monopolise meetings. And nobody says anything! Women are for ever excluded from the social struggle. In those days we were told we had to be patient and wait. Come the revolution there would be crèches, communal canteens, schools for everyone ... they told us all this to calm us down without realising that, in point of fact, they were saying that the caring professions were for women because they were women and that the men would "help" us. Cheers comrade! They said we were separatists and pretended not to realise that the real separatists were themselves. They wanted to see us look pretty, good, and obedient, but they didn't realise they hadn't bought some second hand domestic appliance.

ISABELLA: You, in any case, at the time, you were already an independent woman.

PILAR: Yes, but I paid a heavy price for it. In those days you had to fight against a lot of prejudice and I can assure you that that was not easy. I used to work, I was politically active, I went out at night with friends. Many people spoke badly of me and judged me negatively. When I arrived in France, in 1938, I realised that the condition of women was better than in Spain. I envied those women who had more freedom than us. I wanted to have a political life. I didn't just want to look after my children

ISABELLA: Ken Loach asked you about the status of women in Spain.

PILAR: I consider Ken Loach to be a really interesting cinema director and very sensitive to the political and social reality of our country. He asked me various things about the position of women in society. He wanted to know what we used to get up to, how we dressed, how we spent our time, and what kind of relationship we had with our male comrades, with our party, with the outside world. I told him how I had been to the front to see my partner several times before they killed him. He asked me if there were other women at the front and how they were treated, what type of life they led. There should be more men like him who ask questions about the history of politics and culture. I haven't met many. I hope you are more lucky than I have been.

Conclusions

A collection of interviews is an open book, wanting to be read and handed to a neighbour, available to those who ask questions and to those who give answers, ready to be taken to the beach or even thrown into the sea. I wrote it with all my limitations and the tools I had to hand. And my life became intertwined with that of many other women who helped me grow up and urged me to fight for a better world. I avoided any meticulous historical introduction explaining the difference between anarchist, Francoist, or republican women during the war and the Spanish revolution, and I did not even mention the Cuban revolution, since it is undoubtedly very well known. The words of the protagonists alone provide a historical, human, and personal view of what was their — and hopefully even our — revolution.

Barricades can be found not only on the street — they can also be built and dismantled in our hearts. The women's revolution takes place every day, because everything we do, from morning to night, puts us in contact with the world and with ourselves in the world.

All the women interviewed in this book have given their own stories and if anything is missing hopefully it will stimulate the curiosity of the reader so that they go forward and do their own research. History is not made of "ifs" where things could have been different, instead we should use it as a guide to the future.

My purpose was to archive a historical memory that otherwise would have been lost. Besides war, repression and exile, our greatest enemies are indifference, apathy, and oblivion.

In 1996, I had already completed my historical research on the POUM women and men, but I felt that something was still missing: a focus on the Spanish women but extended to all the women in the world. As best as I could, I moved from Milan to Catalonia. In March 1997, in Barcelona, I met Marta Vergunyos, and she accompanied me to France to carry out my research.

We ended the first series of interviews with Pepita Carpena, Blanca Navarro, and Sara Berenguer, then in Madrid I looked for Suceso Portales and in 2002 I settled down in Peru. In 2008, once back in Europe, I published an oral history book on the POUM and two other autobiographical essays on femicide and my travels to Latin America. I brought along with me the voices of the Spanish revolutionaries whom I had interviewed, during my transoceanic journeys and stays in crumbling houses. I often looked at them in the library of my houses in Cuzco, Lima, Tumbes, Madrid, Barcelona, Bologna, Moscow and Paris, and whenever I had some spare time, I used to work on these texts, but it wasn't easy to translate, transcribe, correct them and find a publishing house willing to support me.

In 2011, with Marta Alier, I looked for Cristina Simónin in the Pyrenees and, with Marta Vergunyos in France, we visited Teresa Rebull and Teresa Carbó who welcomed us into their homes with a hug and a protest song.

Now I felt urged to put an end to this book. Therefore, in order to please them and myself as well, I have finished with the research that you are reading.

Do what you want with it: throw it away like a stone, use it to support a wobbly table in the kitchen or burn it to protect you from the cold but try to honour these women who gave their lives for a dream of love and freedom.

ACKNOWLEDGEMENTS

There are so many women who have urged me to carry out this research, especially the artist Maca'n, who encouraged me to paint the white pages, Marta Vergonyós Cabratosa, who accompanied me during some of the interviews, Marta Alier Fabregó, who welcomed me into her home in Barcelona, and Noemi Santarella, who translated a video-documentary called *De toda la vida* on the anarchist women mentioned in this book.
I would like to thank all of them.

~ **Isabella Lorusso**

Afterword

by **ELISABETH DONATELLO**

Donatello is an educator and communications professional based in Madrid, with a doctorate in Thought and Social Movements.

The women described by Isabella Lorusso look for freedom while others are dazed and empty, locked inside the cage of patriarchal society. The identities imposed on them, outlined here in a detailed manner, are where control, unhappiness and pain linger. They are exemplary stories lived by people who make their decisions, make their own experiences, suffer, get up and fall again in an apparently confused space without any perspective. These stories are unique, different, divergent. They are told in the form of direct dialogues, which give full meaning to the evolving events. These are the lives of those who are able to change in order to lead a full life, taking deep breaths. Challenges faced with courage. With the strength of the limitless force that makes us even more human. It is all meant for us and for the future generations.

Her syntax is contemporary, quick and rich in visual references; made up of short sentences full of meaning and action, able to convey their message with just few words. Isabella puts the human being back in the centre of attention plainly describing the bodies, feelings and intelligence of those who try to discover themselves as well as the beauty of the strong commitment to change the world. The women's bodies are the true protagonists of Isabella's stories. Their incessant movement supports and enhances the underlying feminine thought.

Fighting Women is the latest collection of stories written by Isabella describing her meetings with unique, different, divergent, deeply humanistic women who are constantly searching for something. Stories that have crossed times and places together with Isabella. Towards liberation and freedom.

Isabella writes and her readers see, live, are moved and empathise with her characters. They smell the sour scent, see their trembling chin, recognise the sadness in their eyes, the unique movement of the hand in a human being, which may grab a rifle or caress a face. Among these gestures, so different from one another, life dances, smiles, thinks, meets, listens, loves, smiles, shouts and cries.

Isabella has been travelling for years searching for lives and feelings. At the end of the '90s, in Barcelona, she learnt about distant and old stories. In those years, people mostly discovered stories through dry history books full of dates and events relating to specific groups. I used to put these together, involuntarily depriving the subjects of their humanity as well as of the struggles and stories of the working class, as thought it were a propaganda for the official version requested by the ruling classes to preserve their supremacy. It was a bargaining counter for the granting of a pseudo-democratic regime to a subaltern class, which was no longer regarded as the working class after World War II. Isabella was able to restore that sense of humanity. She does not want just to read. She wants to hear, listen, see, smell, touch and taste first-hand.

Isabella looks for people who belong to an earlier time but are still very much alive. She identifies them one by one in physical places full of meaning and signifiers between the Spanish exile in France and Catalonia. She meets them and talks to them. Isabella asks simple questions and lets them tell their stories. Her vision, as confirmed by those who know her, reflects her inclination towards conversation and human communication, laying the foundations for a free relationship.

Her pressing questions are the voices of those who have sometimes remained silent for more than half a century, hushed and forgotten. Now their lives manifest themselves in the transcription of an oral narration after long meetings recorded among the scents of the houses, places full of fragrances, readings and memories.

The first work published by Isabella, *Voci del POUM (2010)*, was a collection of interviews telling the stories of members of the POUM. Stalin dismantled it, both in Russia and elsewhere, to become the sole leader of the global anti-fascist struggle. The Spanish revolution really tried to change the world in the 20th century, but actually it led to Franco's coup and the 1936-39 civil war. The working class was the actual protagonist of the war, as it wanted to start the desired change. The coup against the Spanish Republic caused an armed struggle. The working class was aware of this and fought to the end in spite of inevitable defeat, abuses and oppression, remaining true to their wish for change.

After the war, being Rojos (red) in Spain under Franco meant you were defined by this regime's pseudoscience as as suffering from a physical-psychological illness, as being the seed of evil, and therefore slaughter was justified. A genocide which was recognised by the UN after World War II, but not by the Spanish state. Mass graves, full of Rojos, were dug only on the initiatives of associations and family members despite the difficulties.

The corpse of Federico García Lorca, immortal and homosexual poet and playwright, has never been found. The Rojos were subjected to torture, retaliation, violence and abuse, especially women. The Church, the army and the middle classes could not accept feminist liberation. The oppression of women was one of the pillars of Franco's regime, which wanted to avoid the education of children and the transmission of memory among the members of the same families and, to this end, took the children away from Rojas mothers and had them adopted by supporters of the regime, who committed to teaching them Francoist ideas. This was a real obsession too among the dictatorships of Latin America. It is no coincidence that the liberation and the preservation of the memory of these horrible crimes by the dictatorships — such as in Argentinia — was connected to the women's relentless struggle urging the post-Junta state to publish the truth, with the purpose of serving justice for those who were subjected to the dictatorship's brutality. The massive exile of the Spaniards to Latin America in the '30s bore fruit here. In fact, a trial for genocide against Francoism and its living members responsible for those atrocious crimes is being conducted precisely in Argentina. Still looking for tierra y libertad. The thread linking us to Spain then still exists today and must be shared.

Isabella reported the stories of the women and men of the POUM with a novel narrative style. She did not remove the story of women, as the patriarchal historiographies used to. She preserved the subjectivity of the story and conveyed their voice in a direct narration made up of her questions and the answers of those who experienced the Spanish social revolution first-hand. This structure is horizontal and rich in the emotions that represent the true intelligence of the people. Their lives, deeply marked by these tragic events, are respectable and rich, with the wild willingness to defend any just cause which further enriches the narration. After those incredible years the then "very young protagonists" of the revolution have never given up their struggle for a better world, wherever they were.

Isabella recovered these stories, which were covered by the ruins of a war that, in spite of the defeat and the inability to find the corpses, has not overcome them. They were killed, banished, persecuted, hushed, forgotten and overlooked by the historical reconstruction of the ruling class which did not want to give the floor to them and listen to their words. These stories had been regarded as old, useless and unattractive, as they deal with a defeat.

Isabella, however, reporting their words. Then she found out that these men and women had been desperately waiting for someone willing to listen to them and to tell their stories. They all adhered to popular movements with the purpose of changing the world, and they succeeded, in different times and ways, depending on the similarities and the various social-political forms, introducing a real transformation of the Spanish society which culminated with the triumph of a popular front for the first time at the general elections (of 2015).

Memories build up our visions, ideas and the utopias, which are brought back to life and gain a new strength. A good example is the search of these Spaniards for a better world, which has inspired other struggles. These stirrings are the same all over the globe, wherever the oppressed people wanted (and still want) a fairer world based on solidarity, sharing and civil coexistence among human beings characterised by the same action and thought processes. There are no boundaries: the oppressed peoples recognise each other and join forces. The Spanish revolution benefited from an unprecedented international attention, as it was intended as the defence of a new-born society model which recognised itself as such. Those revolutionaries described themselves as men fighting the same struggle in the strong belief that el Pueblo Unido jamás será vencido.

Isabella has spent many years on travelling since that early work working among different communities, and has continued to write and tell stories with growing pleasure and proficiency. She involves the readers in her experiences, sharing with them the lives about which she learned from time to time. Time gives strength to our ideas, which are able to survive in spite of the life hardships. This is what happened to Isabella and the other women described by her.

She is a woman writing about women, stressing the contradictions and inequalities in every place and among any community: feminist struggles that turn into social revolution with the purpose of reaching the highest form of emancipation from any oppression. Without liberation from the patriarchal model no revolution can occur and only the same forms are perpetuated. And so in *Fighting Women* Isabella returns to re-interview and expand on the women she had interviewed in the '90s. She feels the need to tell their stories.

This work has previously been published in Italian and Spanish, as *Donne Contro* (2014) and *Mujeres en Lucha* (2019). It is a collective book, the women belonging to different social-political groups but sharing the same struggle for women's emancipation intended to liberate humanity from any oppression, a step necessary to break the totalitarian system at the root of patriarchy. This convergence of otherwise politically-divergent voices by Isabella helps us to clearly distinguish unifying lines throughout the narrative process.

Isabella doesn't just tells stories, she and her subjects and teach us about how we can do it ourselves, learning through unmediated voices telling of their memories, decisions and responsibilities. She and her interviewees remind us that we must renew our just struggle for women and their rights, in the hope that it helps future generations. We must all get rid of the chains of oppression, which have been created by the ruling classes belonging to patriarcal and capitalist systems.

> Lucho was a guerrilla and a great poet as well. He told me that one of his comrades was killed by a policeman on March 8th while she was occupying the canteen of a factory. "She fell right in front of me, but we had to flee, we were surrounded by the policemen who were shooting at us". He told me her story and hugged me. "She was a fierce feminist, the look in your eyes reminds me of her, I'll never forget her".
> ~ Isabella Lorusso, *Otokongo*, Ibiskos ed, page 58

Even when we make no progress and are defeated by the events, even when we fall back and suffer from horrible pains, the ideas are still there, manifest themselves and become ours, strengthened by the strong example of those who have already expressed them. If even the oppression of invisibility, the hardest thing to bear, can be broken, then today we all must follow this path, comforted and supported by the words of these great women who changed the world and never stopped fighting. They waited for decades for the possibility of telling their stories. And we will never know how hard it was to wait for such a long time for recognition.

The strength of this book lies in its ability to show that we can and must go on, always with our heads held high, even when everything around us seems to be lost and governed by a hegemonic supremacy. Going on, moving in new directions rather than following roads chosen by our oppressors.

> The orangutan came out slamming the door and my mother cried desperately: "You're a bitch! Why didn't you tell him that you would leave anything to him, why? You're a damned feminist! He is a man, don't you understand?"
> ~ Isabella Lorusso, T1/3 page 26 in T1/3
> *Storia di un femminicidio*, Ibiskos ed.

Isabella and the other women tell us that we must not agree to become invisible. We must not allow anyone to stop and ridicule our lives, ideas and skills as women. We must not leave any woman to struggle alone.

We must not passively adapt to the stereotypes imposed on us by oppressors both in the public and in the private sphere. We must be sympathetic and always ready to join forces, gather, share our ideas and experiences, and look for other solutions and paths. We must participate in public life and break the terrible chains of the patriarchal violence with the help of those movements that struggle for a change.

Isabella and the other women talk about contraception, abortion, divorce, labour and family rights, acting and educating in new, different and divergent ways. They talk about the political meetings and the collective readings, backed up by evening classes after a day of work in the factory. Those readings — which were never individual, but rather collective, sharing the contents and reflections — turned them into the protagonists of the struggle, strengthening their identity against the machismo of the comrades and against the self-righteous and sanctimonious middle-class society. They started a path of liberation which has sets a good example.

Isabella and the other women will always be there for us, to give us strength and energy whenever we are about to suffocate, whenever we are about to give up.

The stories told by Isabella can deeply change the world of the reader. Let this change begin and share this experience with another human being. This is the only possible future for mankind. This is the only way to break the horrible chain of imposed pain which binds us. This is the only way to establish a network of solidarity and sharing through words and human relations. This is the only true, full, possible freedom. The freedom of humanity.

Thanks to Isabella who writes, travels, tells stories and smiles.
Thanks to the other women who have been able to wait for the possibility of telling their stories.
Thanks to those who are never fed up with reading, talking, sharing, fighting, changing.
Thanks to those who live their life dancing and singing, always willing to try every move.
The true spring of our time is on the way.

~ **Elisabeth Donatello**

ABOUT FREEDOM PRESS

The oldest anarchist publishing house in the English speaking world, Freedom Press was founded in London by Charlotte Wilson and Peter Kropotkin in 1886. A major player in British anarchist politics at the turn of the 20th century, publishing writers including Italian firebrand Errico Malatesta and historian Max Nettlau, it fell into decline in the 1920s before being revived by a group of anti-war activists in the 1930s.

The Press briefly became famous in a 1945 free speech case, when the editors of its journal *War Commentary* were arrested and tried for writing anti-State and anti-war essays causing "disaffection in the armed forces". Although an all-star cast of advocates rallied to defend them, including Herbert Read, George Orwell, Benjamin Britten and E M Forster, all but one were jailed.

Post-war, Freedom was revived by a group formed around Vernon Richards. While Richards was sometimes a controversial figure the Press brought a number of successful writers and artists into its circles during his nearly 60 years as a publisher, including works by Marie-Louise Berneri, Clifford Harper, Donald Rooum and Colin Ward among many others.

Based in the heart of London, Freedom is often on the front line of major events and has been firebombed twice by fascists, in 1993 and 2013. On both occasions the Press was saved by immense solidarity from the global anarchist movement.

Today Freedom Press runs Britain's largest anarchist bookshop at its home of more than 50 years in Whitechapel, and continues to regularly publish works on the philosophy and activities of anarchists. We run a daily anarchist news site at freedomnews.org.uk and continue to publish a free bi-annual printed journal, *Freedom*.

The full fascinating story of its 134-year history is told in *A Beautiful Idea* by Rob Ray (ISBN 978-1904491309), available from the Freedom Bookshop in Angel Alley, London and online at freedompress.org.uk.

ALSO BY THE PUBLISHER

The May Days: Barcelona 1937
by Augustin Souchy, Jose Peirats, Burnett Bolloten and Emma Goldman
Most academics treat the May Days in Barcelona 1937 as "a minor incident in the Spanish Civil War" in spite of the fact that casualties – 500 killed and 1,000 wounded – were actually greater that in the first week of the military uprising in Barcelona.
£5.95 | 126pp | ISBN: 978-0-900384-39-5

Workers in Stalin's Russia
by Marie Louise Berneri
Using the original propaganda of the Soviet system itself, Berneri's scalpel-sharp dissection demonstrates that socialism did not exist in the USSR and shows how the lives of its workers were essentially the same as for those who lived under capitalist democracies.
Coming November 2020 | ISBN: 978-1-904491-36-1

Anarchism is Movement
by Tomás Ibáñez
Ibáñez grew up in France as the child of anarchist refugees in the aftermath of the Spanish Civil War. Joining the CNT in exile, he was active through Paris 1968 and returned to Spain as Franco's grip loosened in 1973. Now, after a lifetime of struggle, AIM distils his thought and predictions on anarchism in times to come, considering its renaissance in Spain and elsewhere.
£7.50 | 138pp | ISBN: 978-1-904491-33-0

BUY ONLINE AND IN PERSON

Freedom relies on volunteer labour and takes low profits on its books in an effort to make them available to working people at the lowest price possible. As a result we mostly use+ income from our bookshop in Whitechapel to cover everyday costs such as utilities and business rates.

In an era where Amazon has largely built a monopoly in publishing we do not stock our books there and are committed to helping radical bookshops survive, as members of the Alliance of Radical Booksellers (radicalbooksellers.co.uk). We strongly encourage readers to buy from the outlets listed there, or from us direct, even if it means Jeff Bezos has only enough money to stack it halfway to the Moon.

You can find our physical shop at the address below, and we stock all our titles, plus many more both obscure and less so, via our online store. Just head over to:

freedompress.org.uk

FINDING FREEDOM

Address:
Freedom Bookshop,
Angel Alley,
84b Whitechapel High Street,
London
E1 7QX

The nearest **Tube** station is Aldgate East (Whitechapel Gallery exit) on the District and Hammersmith & City lines.

Buses: 25, 205 and 254 stop nearby.

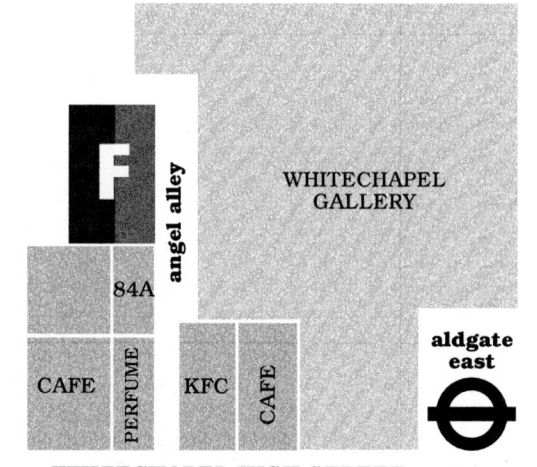